Ashley's Adult Coloring Book

By Ashley Audette

Color Pallet

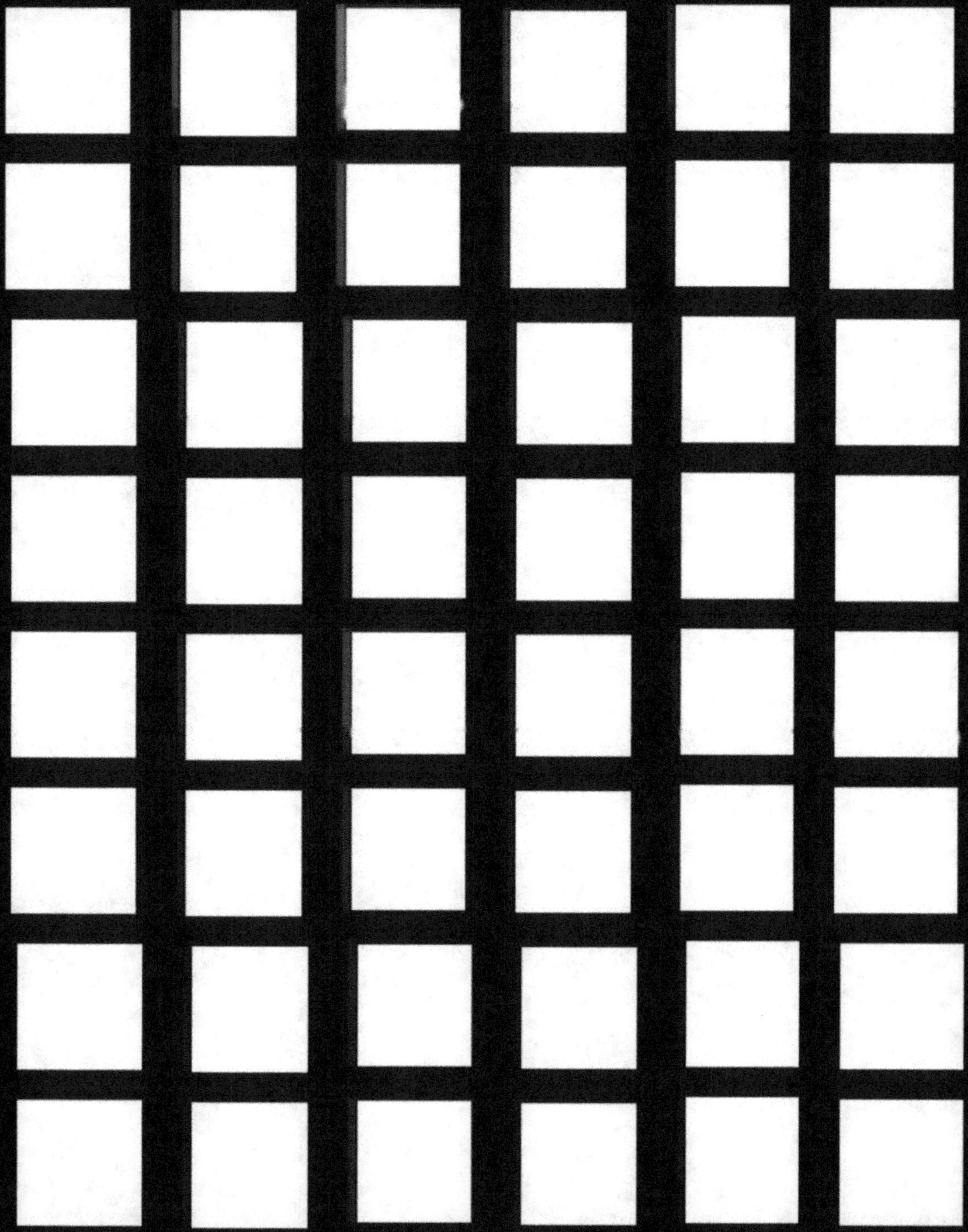

Color Pallet

Color Pallet

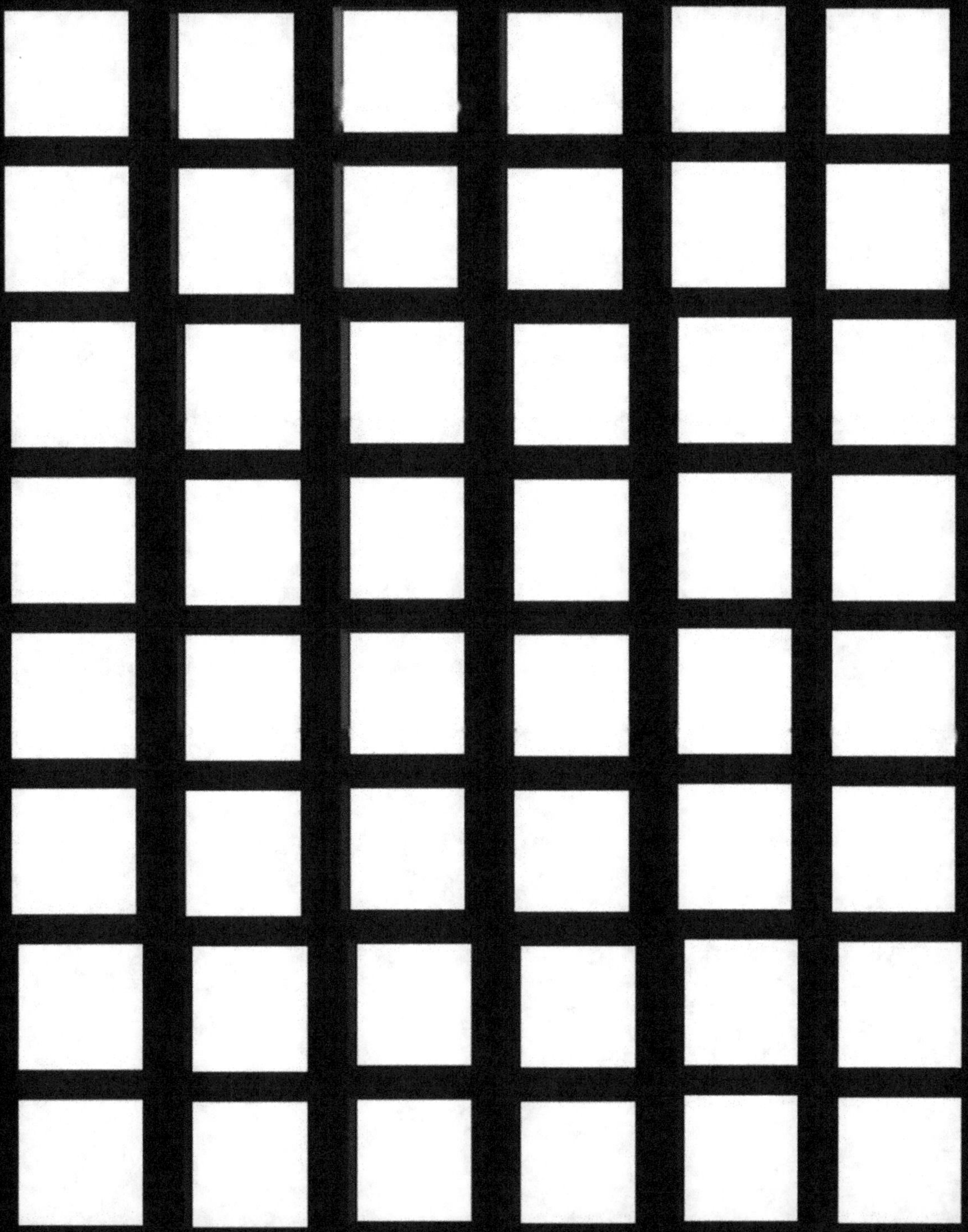

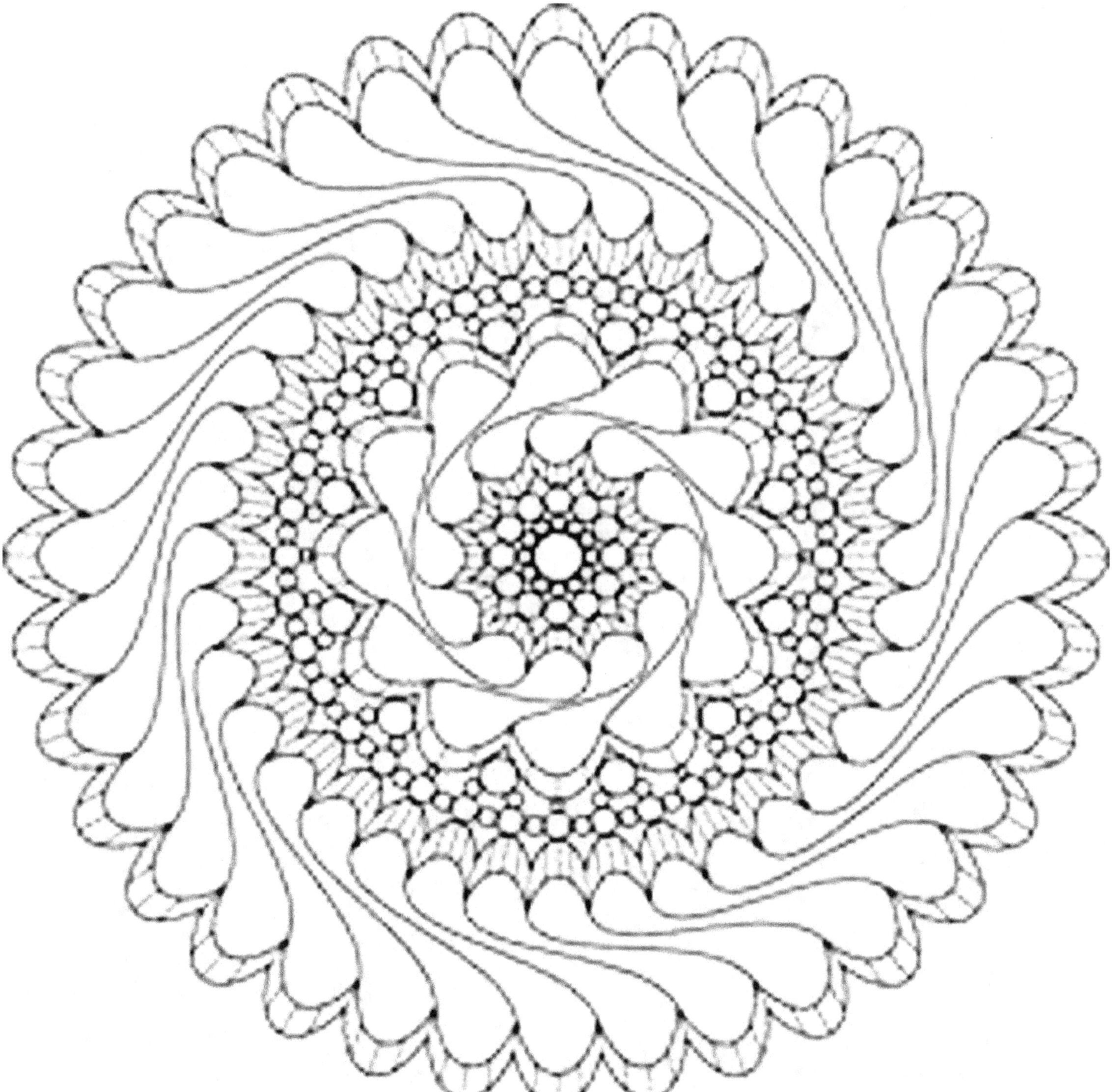

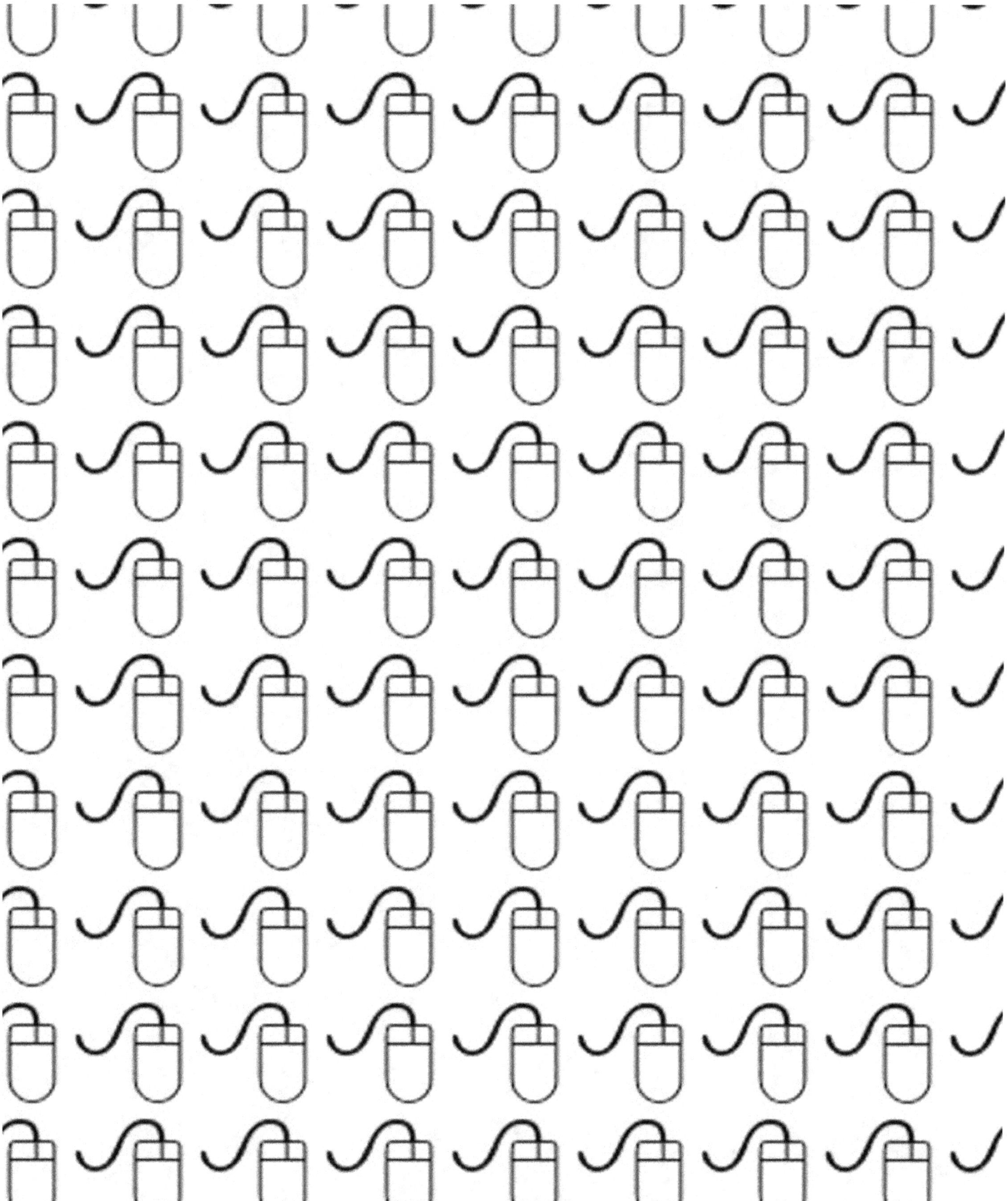

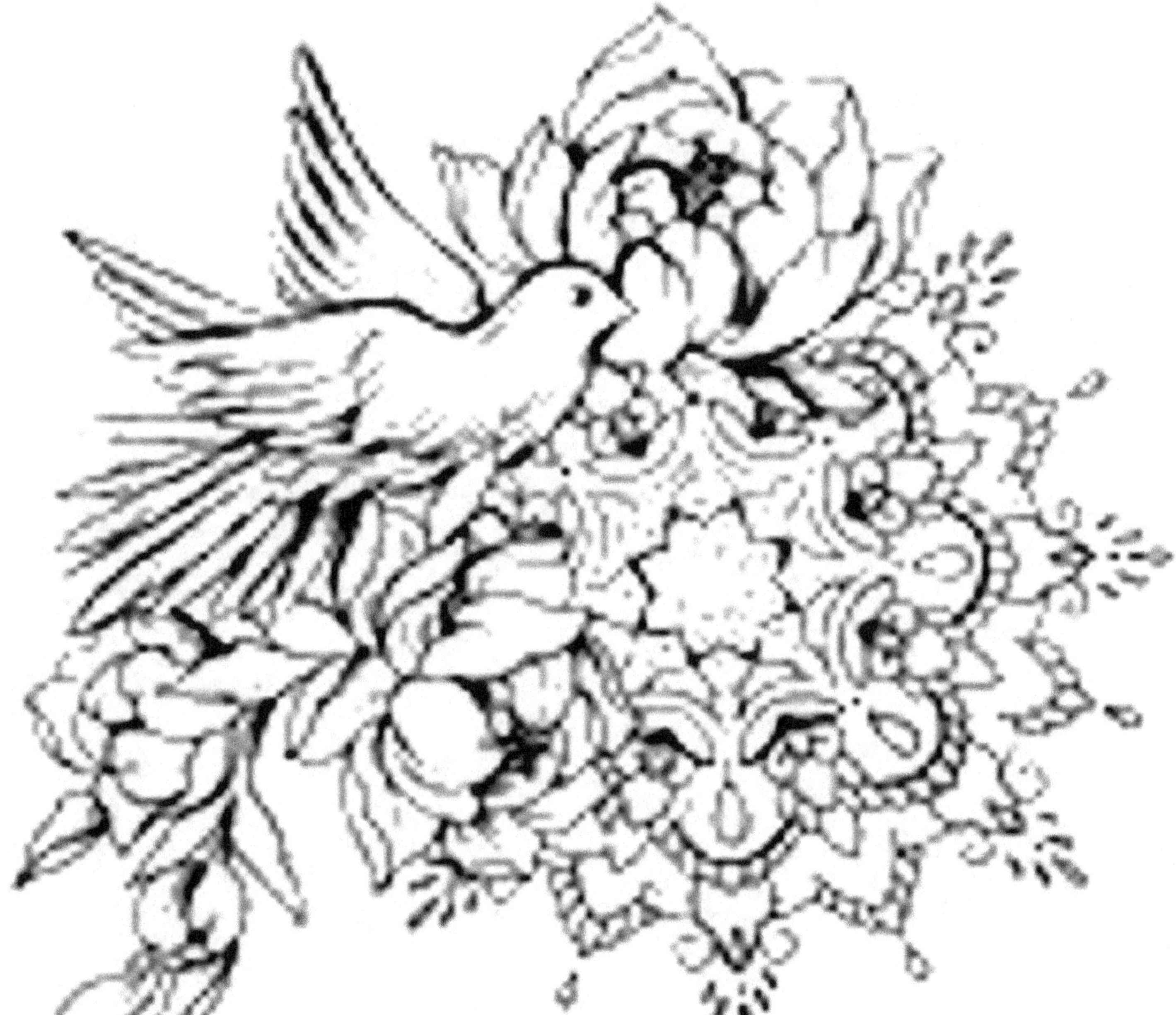

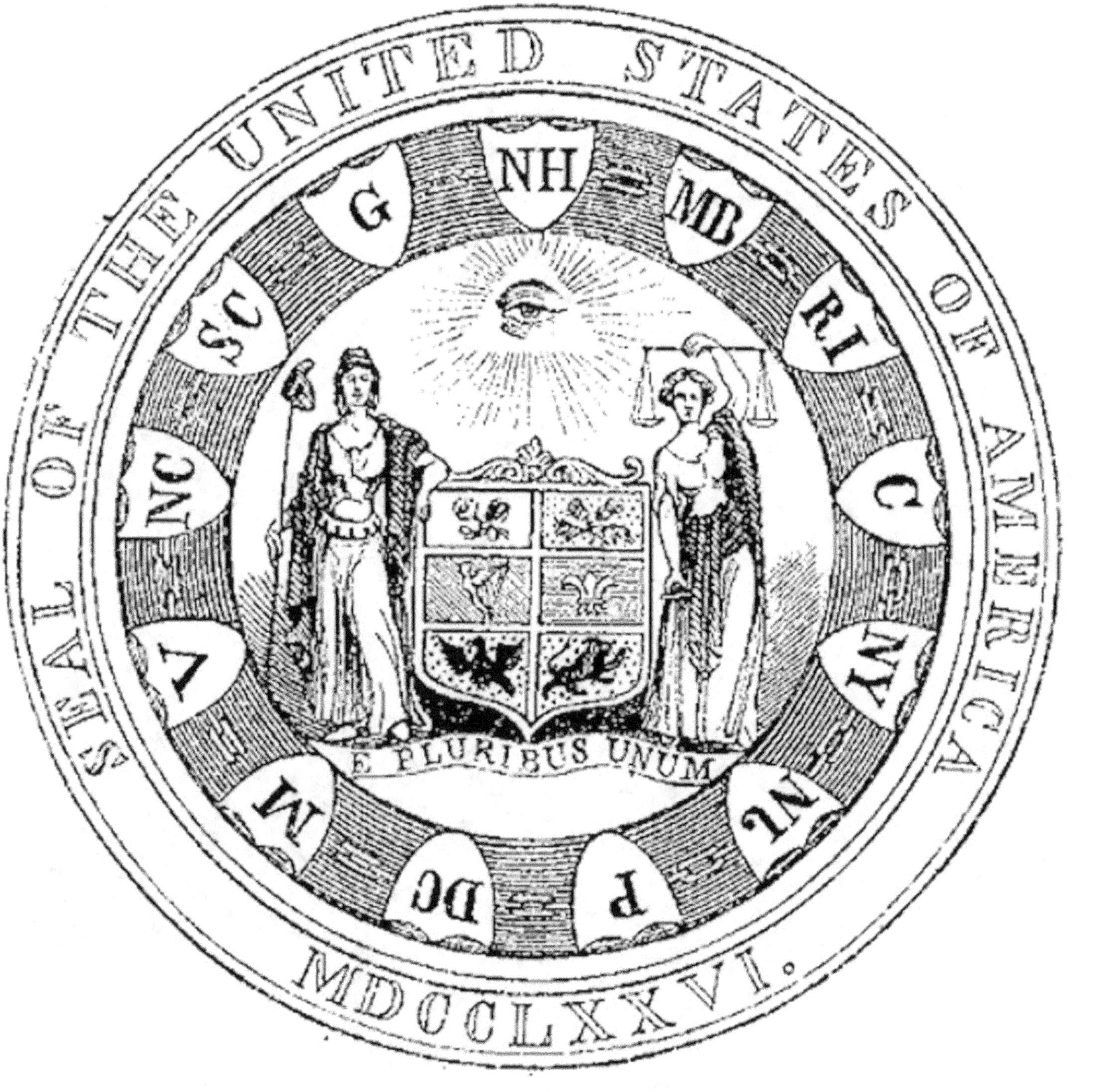
SEAL OF THE UNITED STATES OF AMERICA
NH
MB
RI
C
NY
NJ
P
DC
M
V
NC
SC
G
E PLURIBUS UNUM
MDCCLXXVI.

DIEU ET MON DROIT

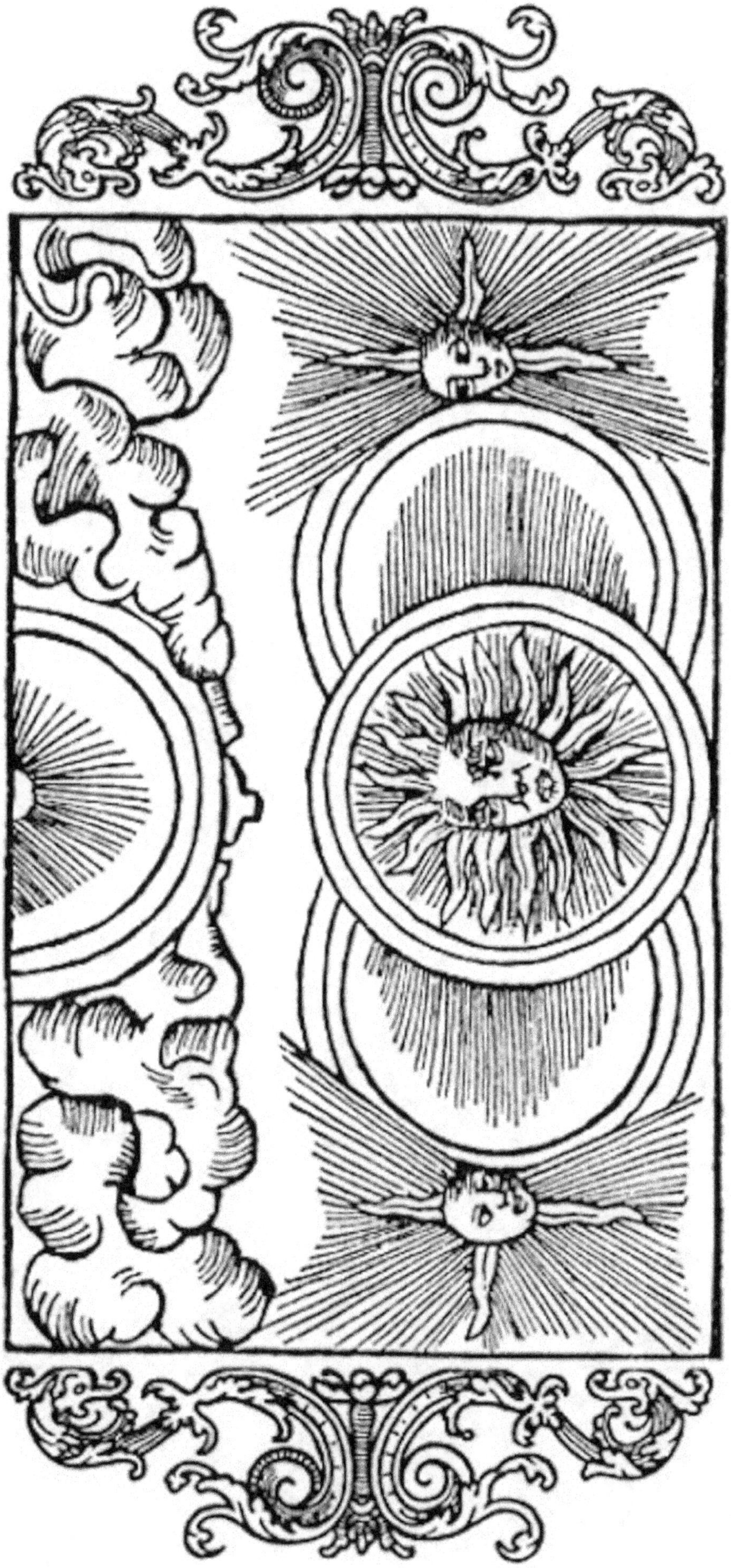

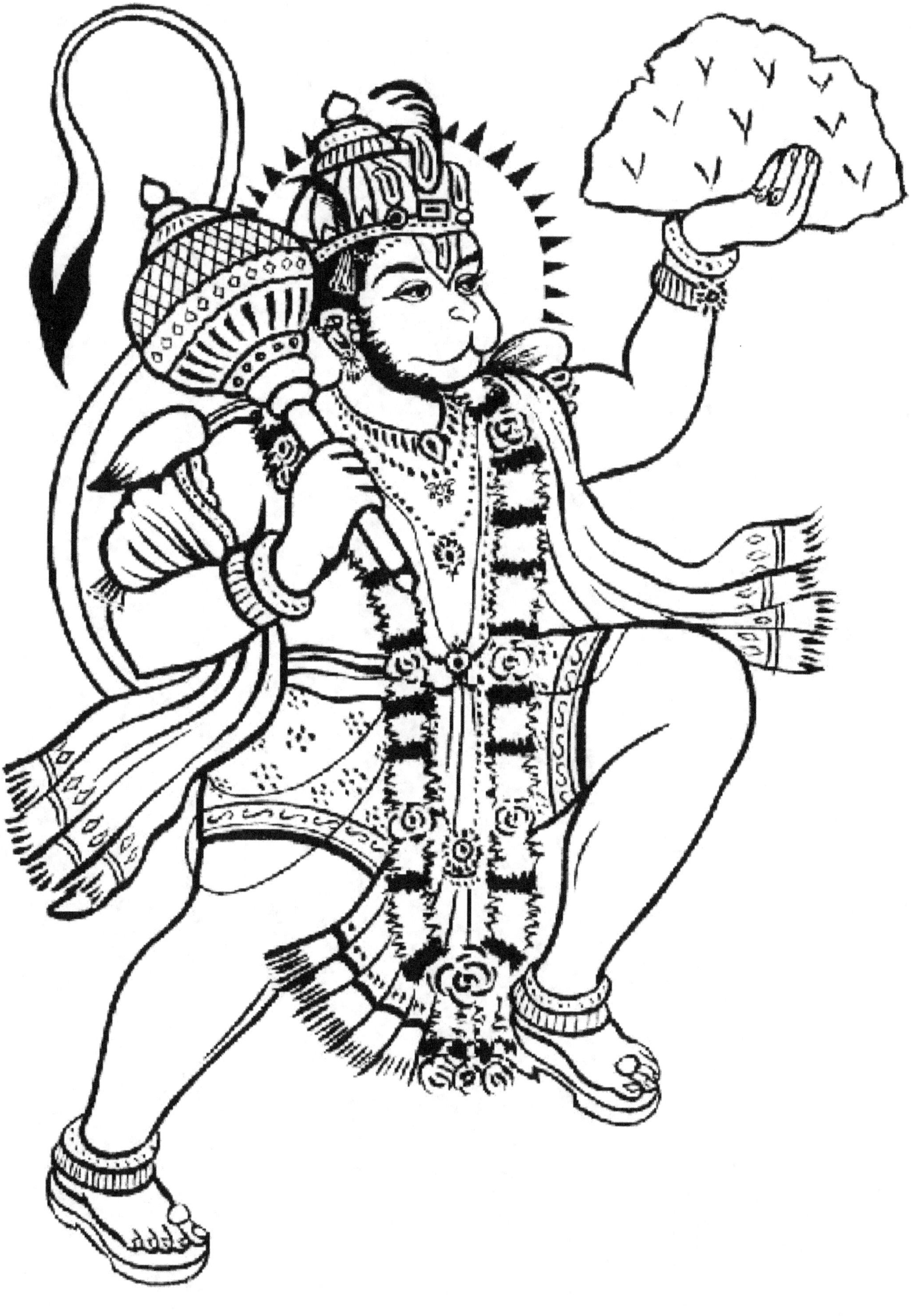

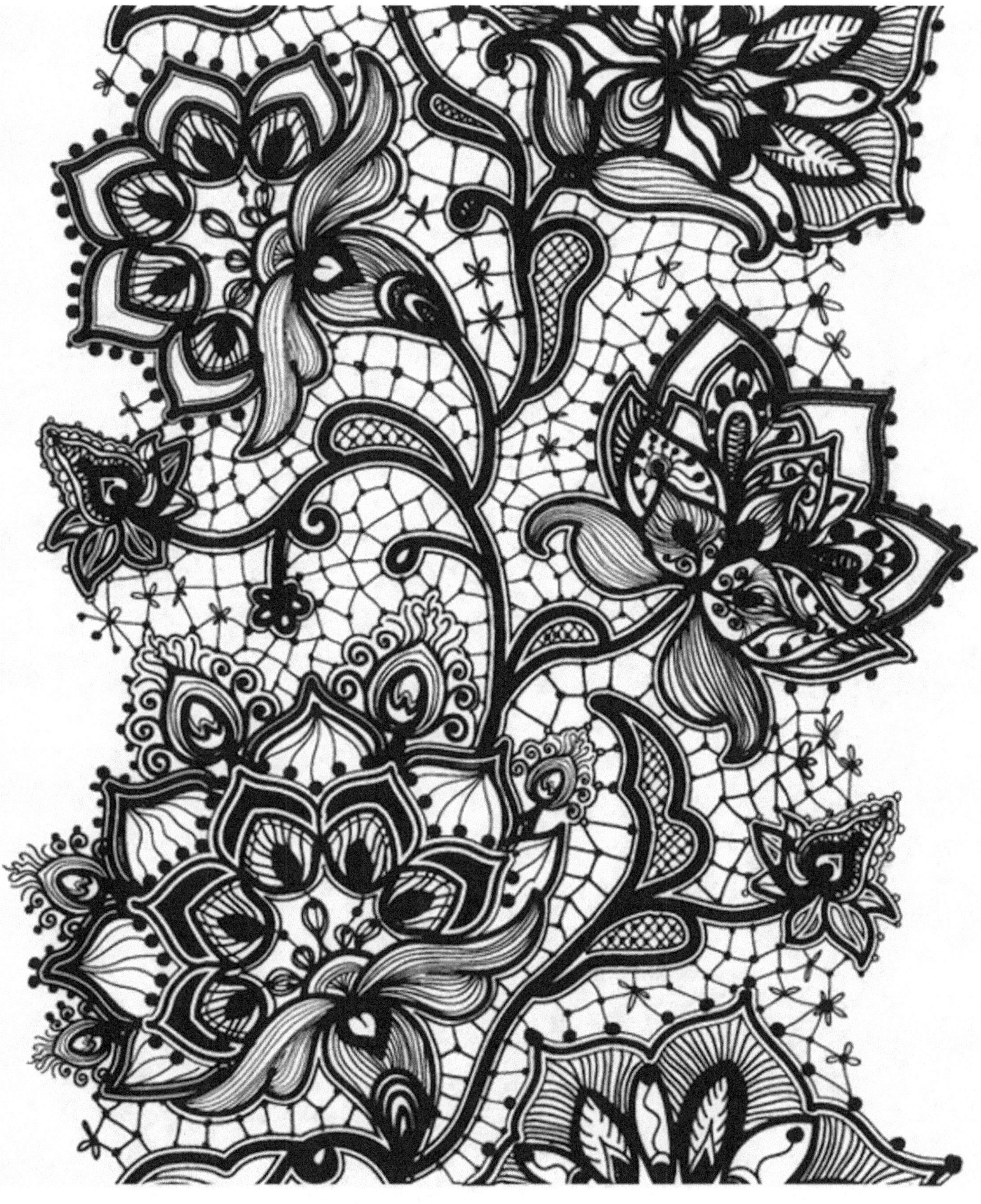

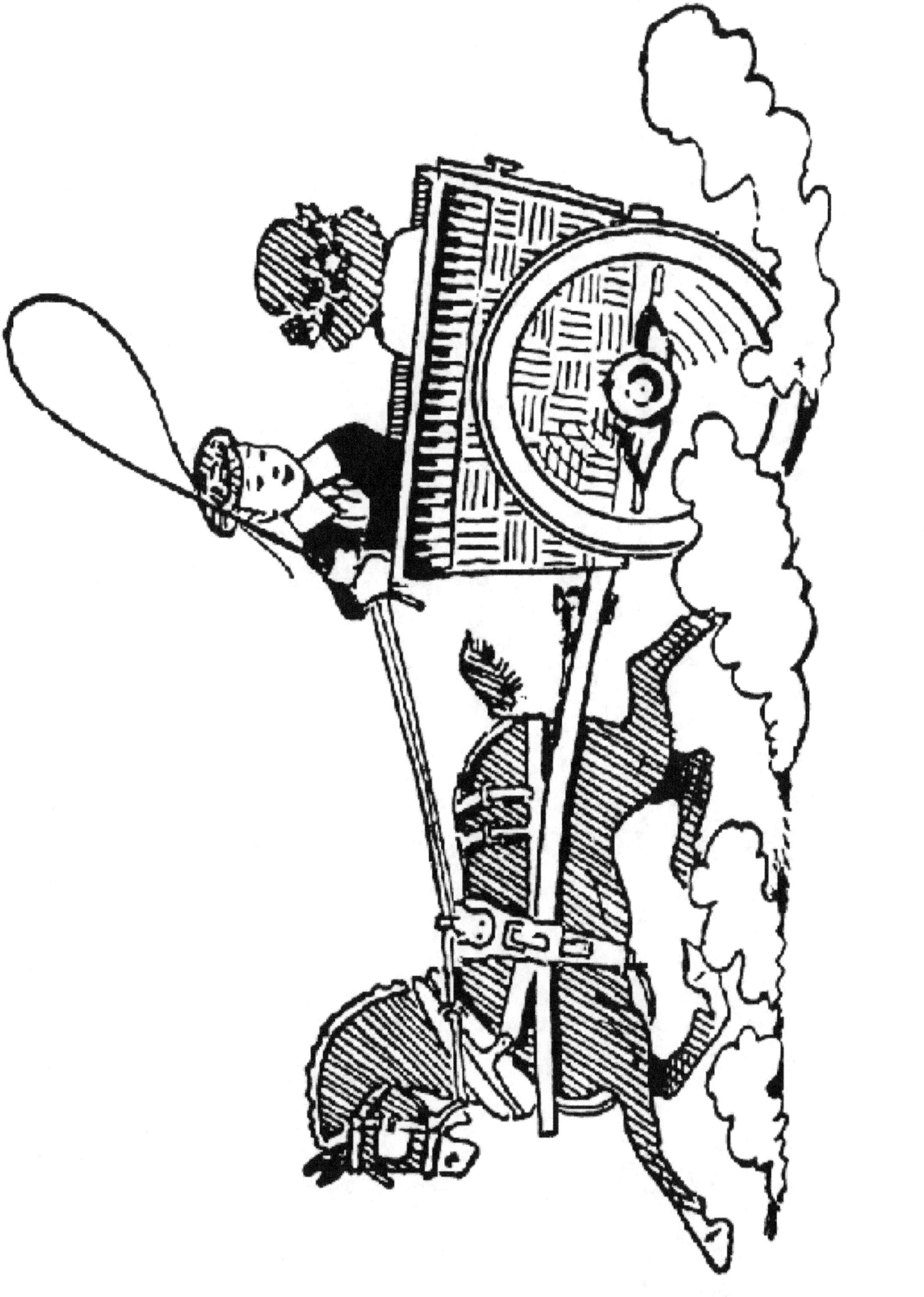

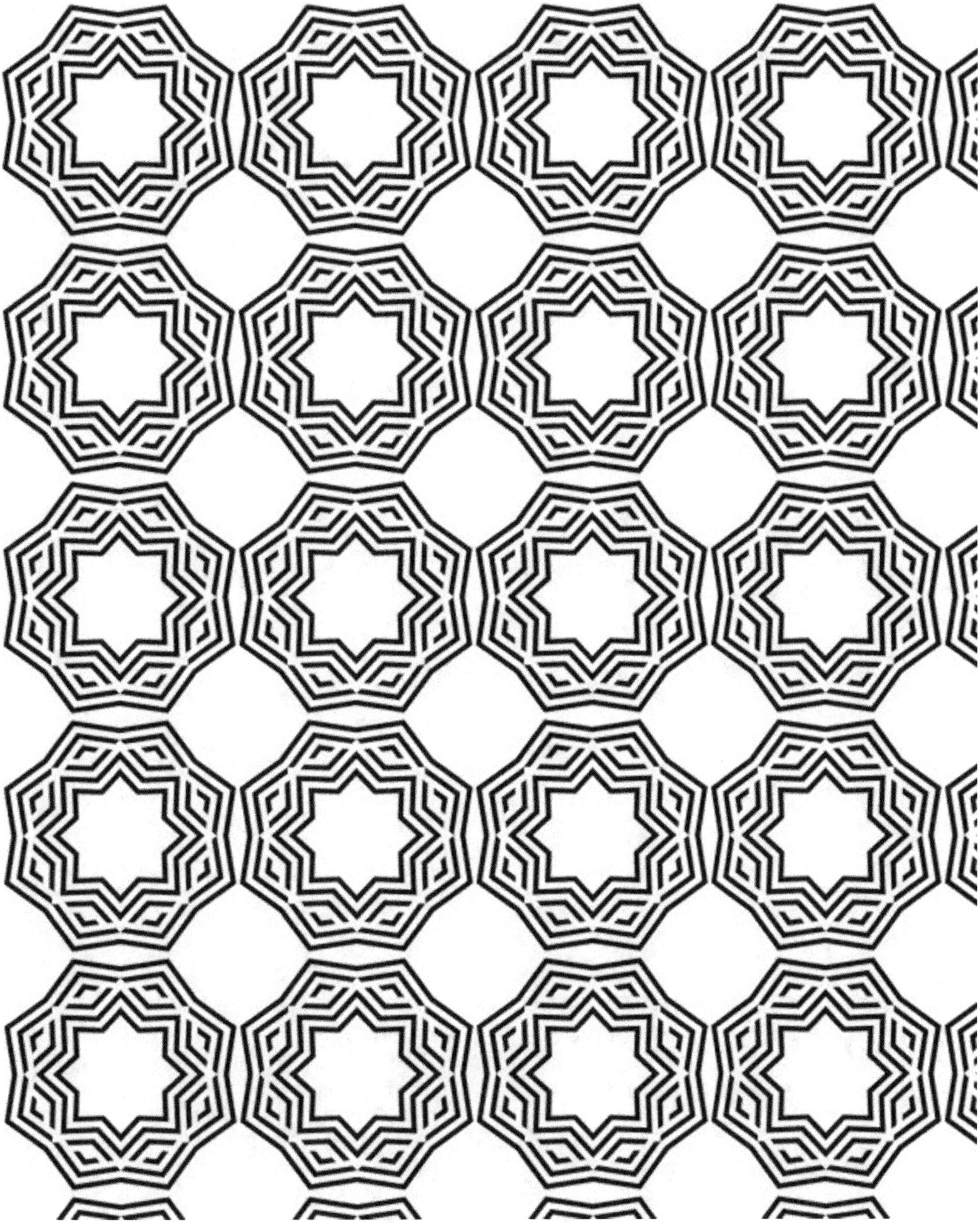

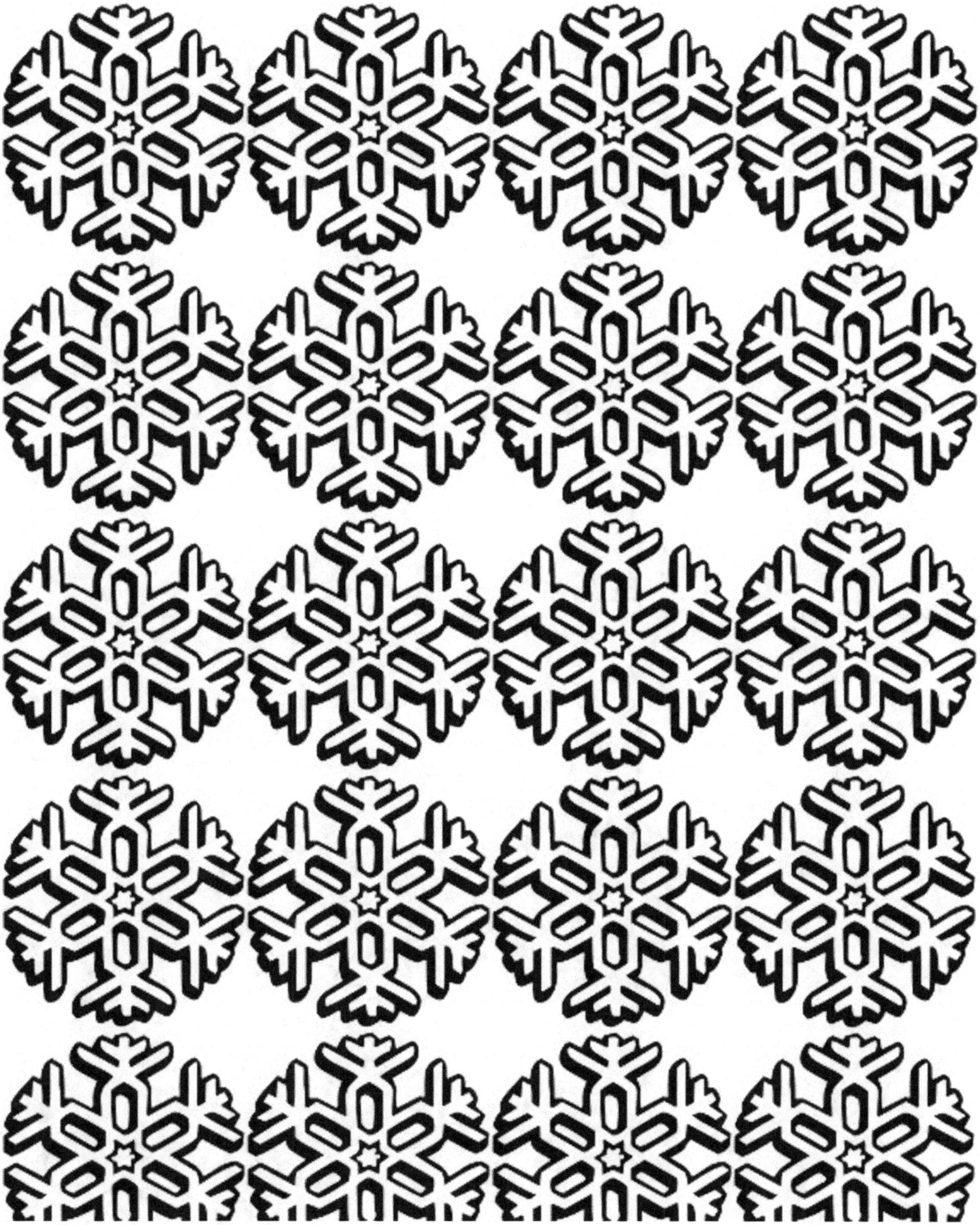

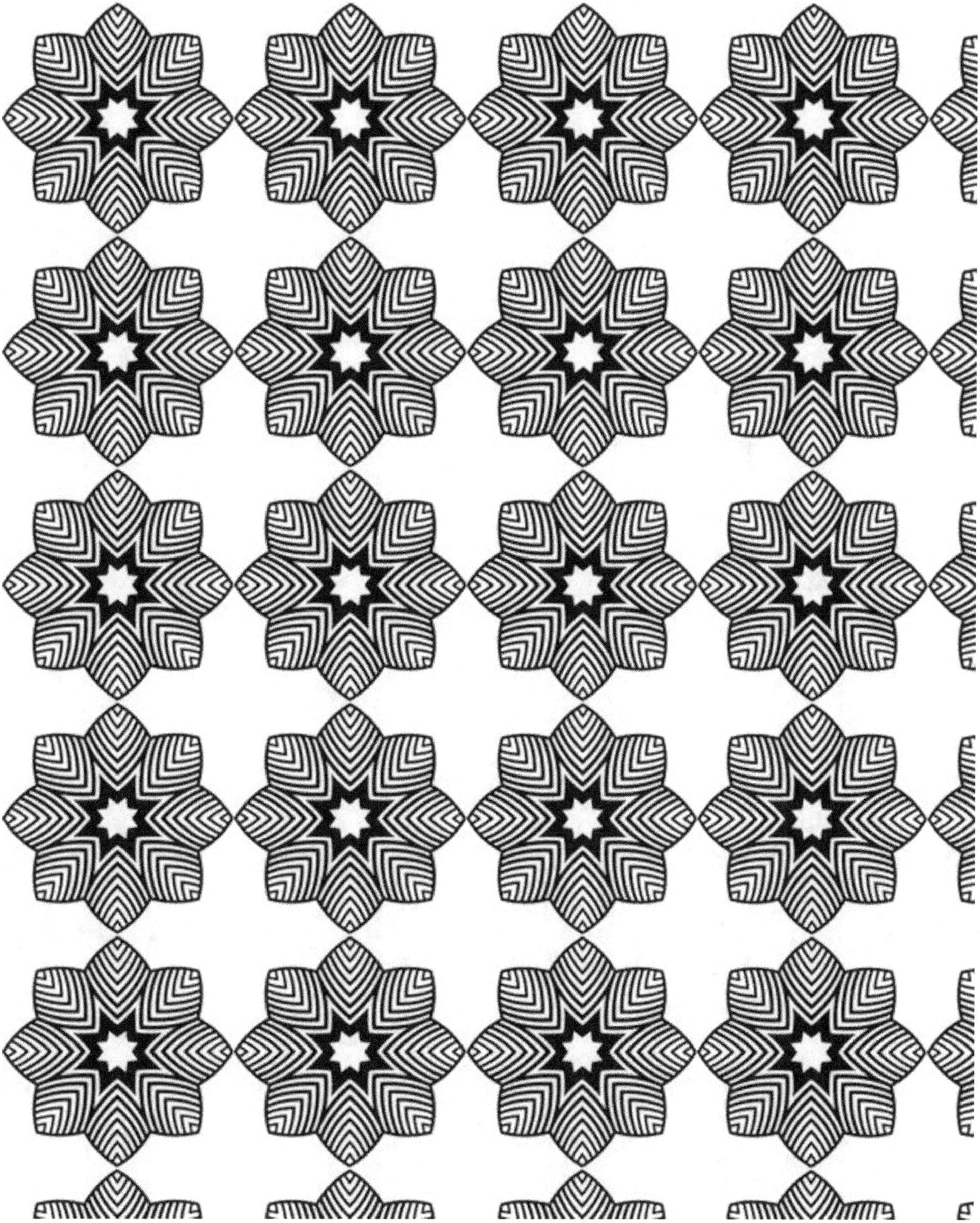

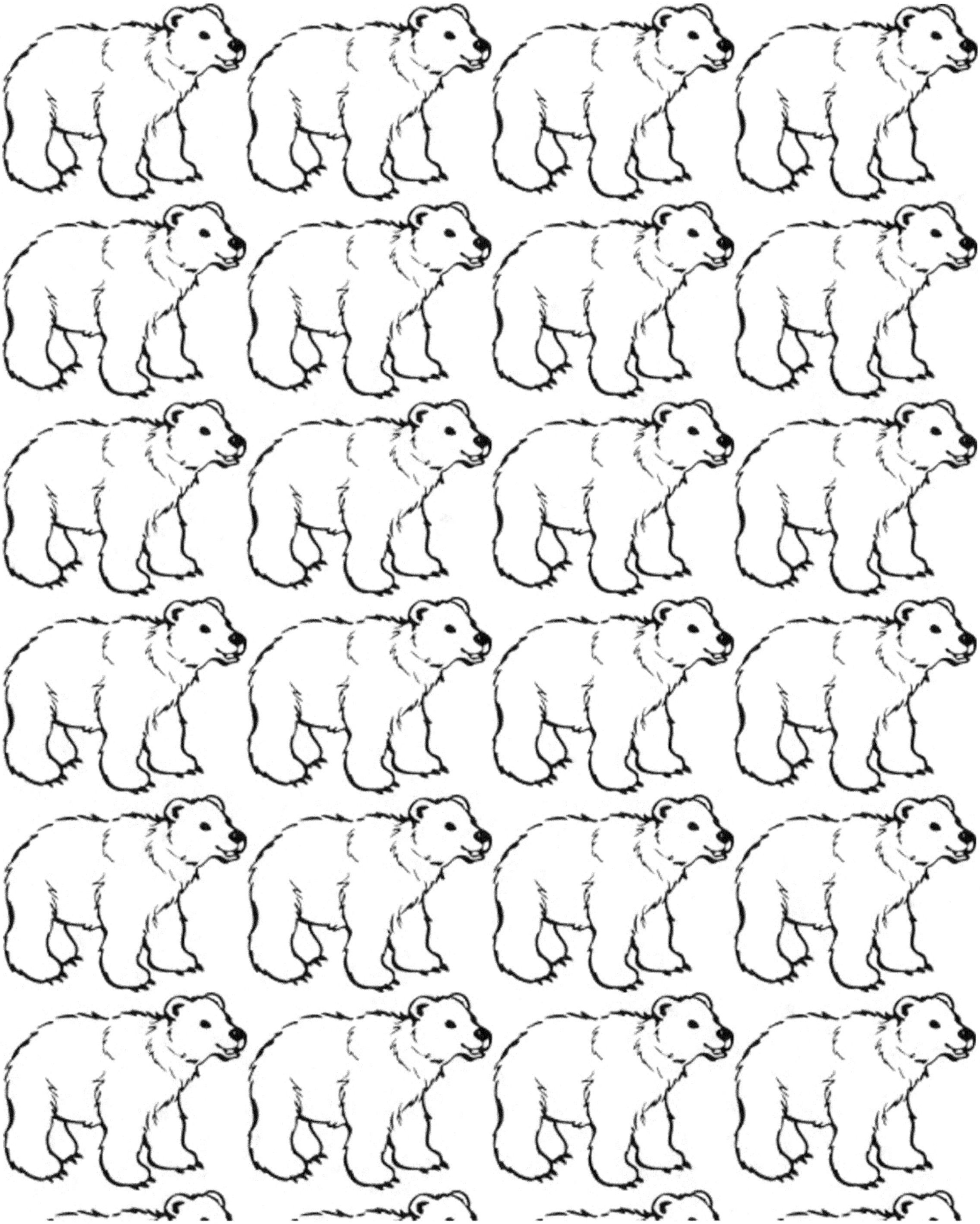

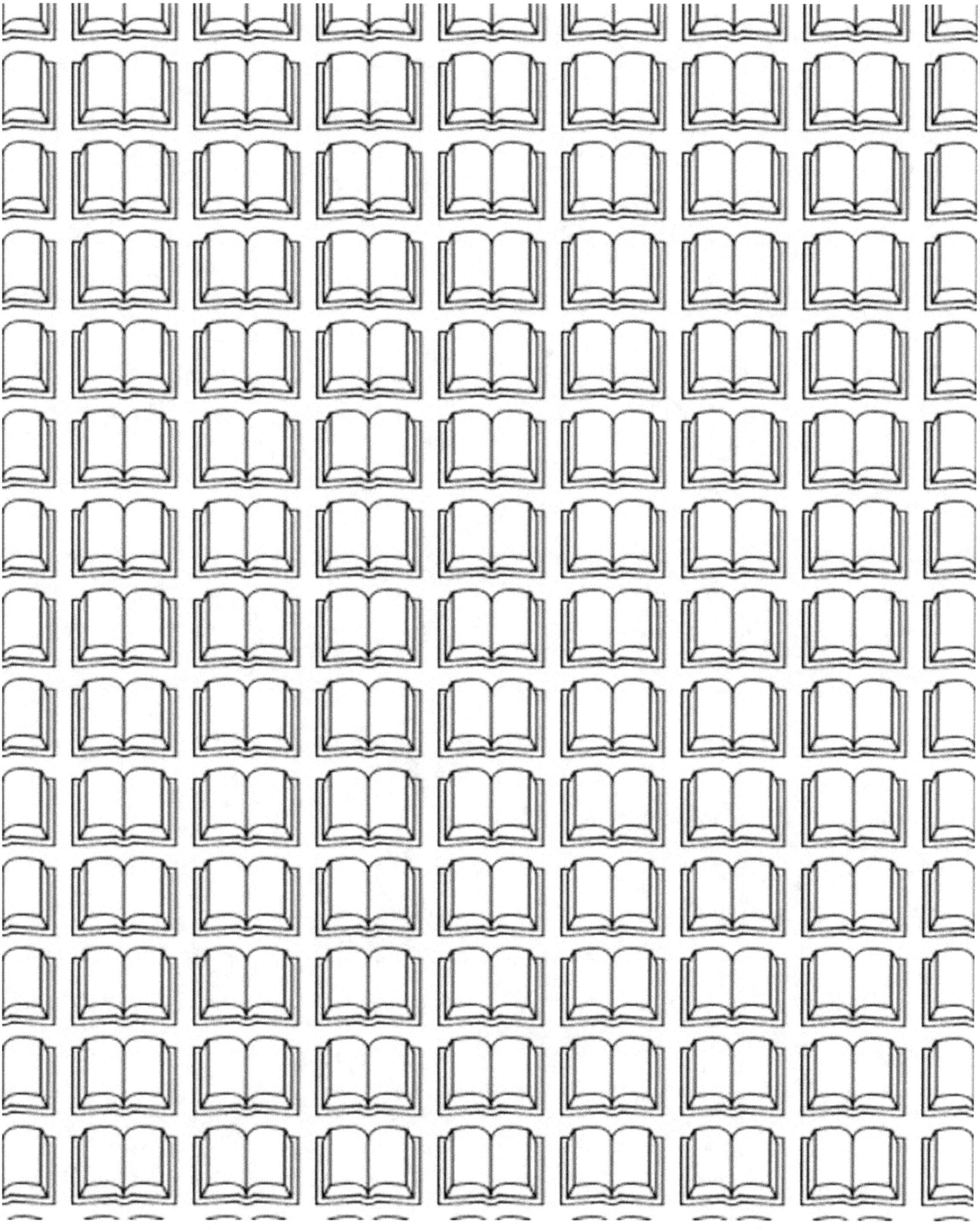

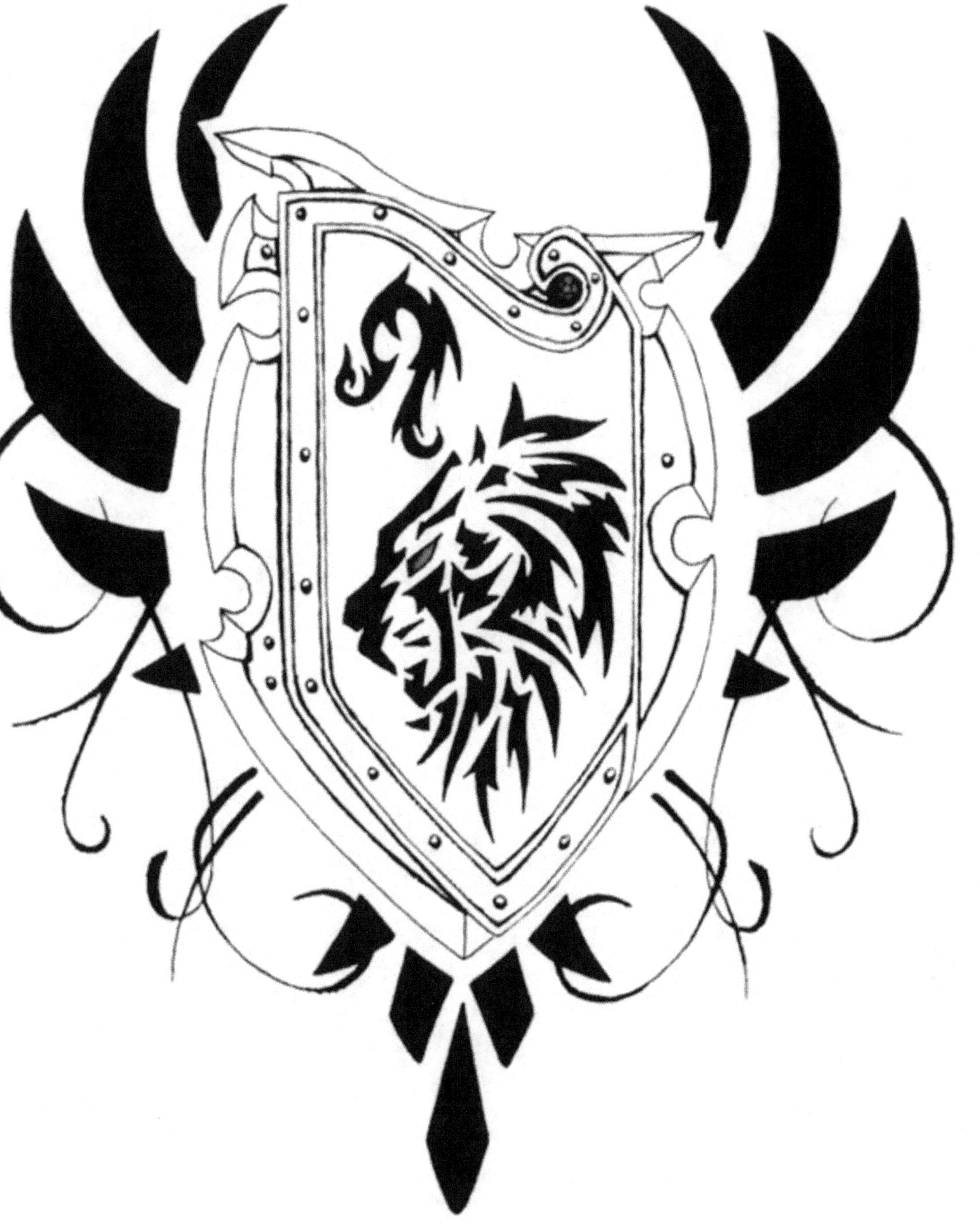

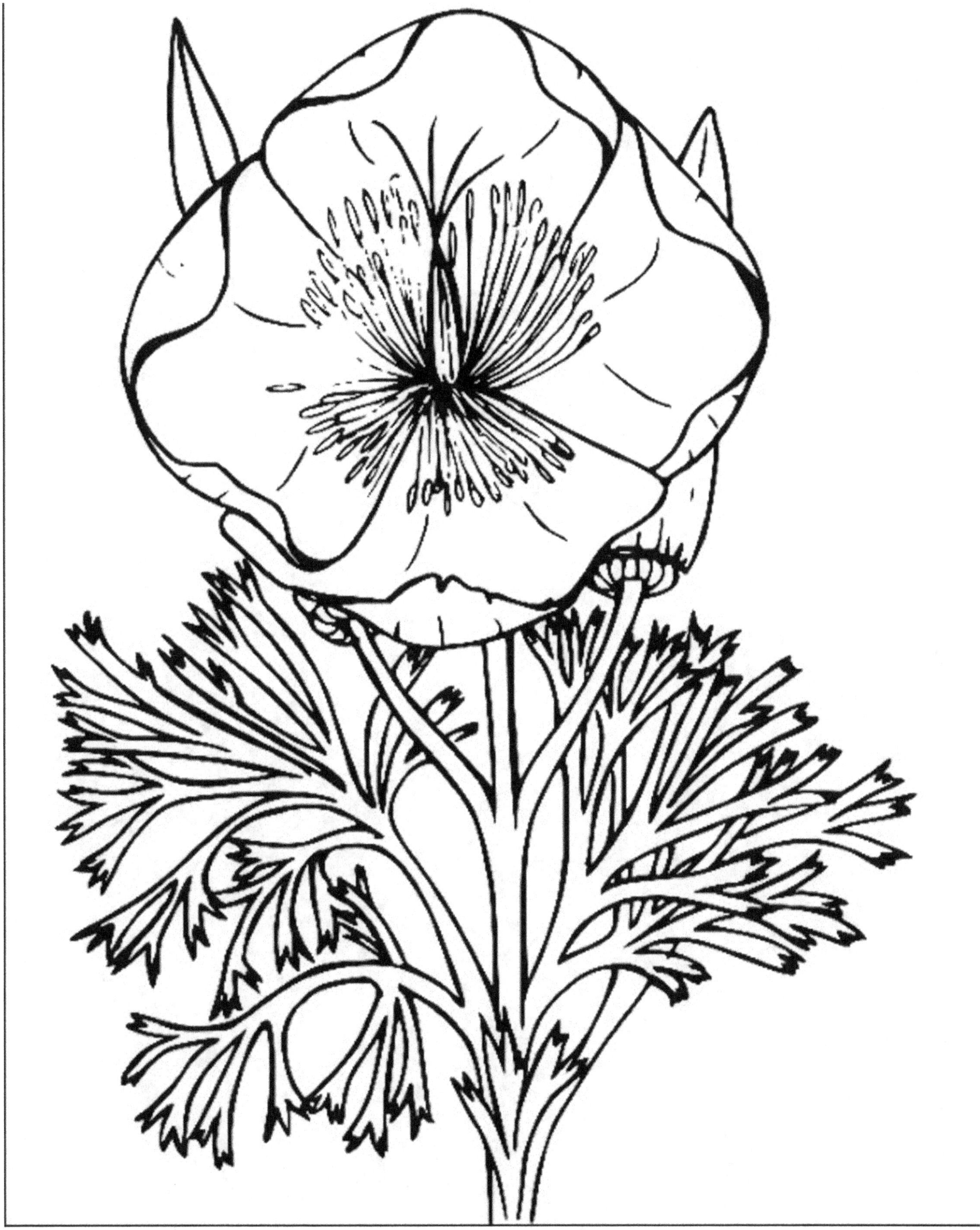

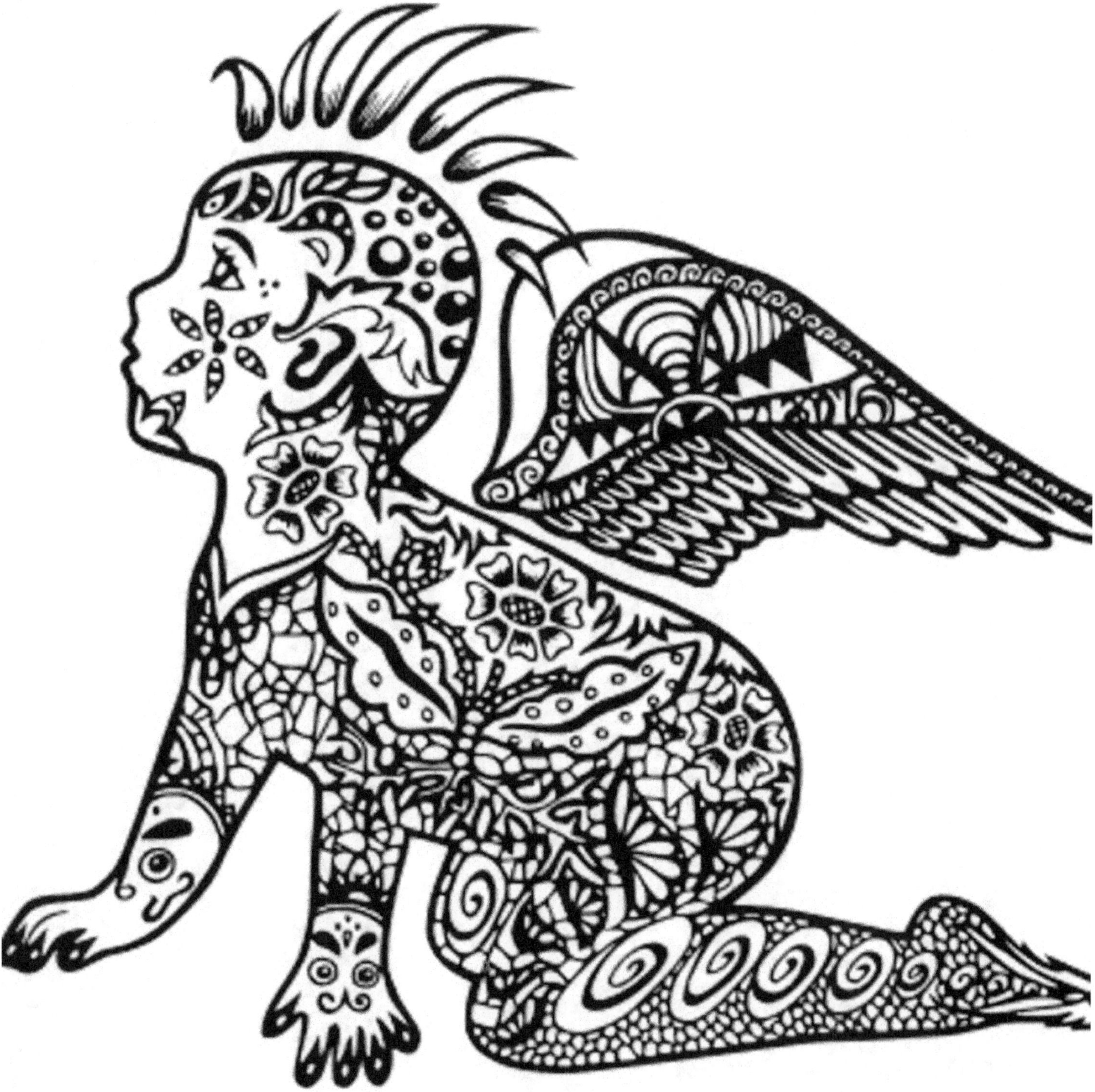

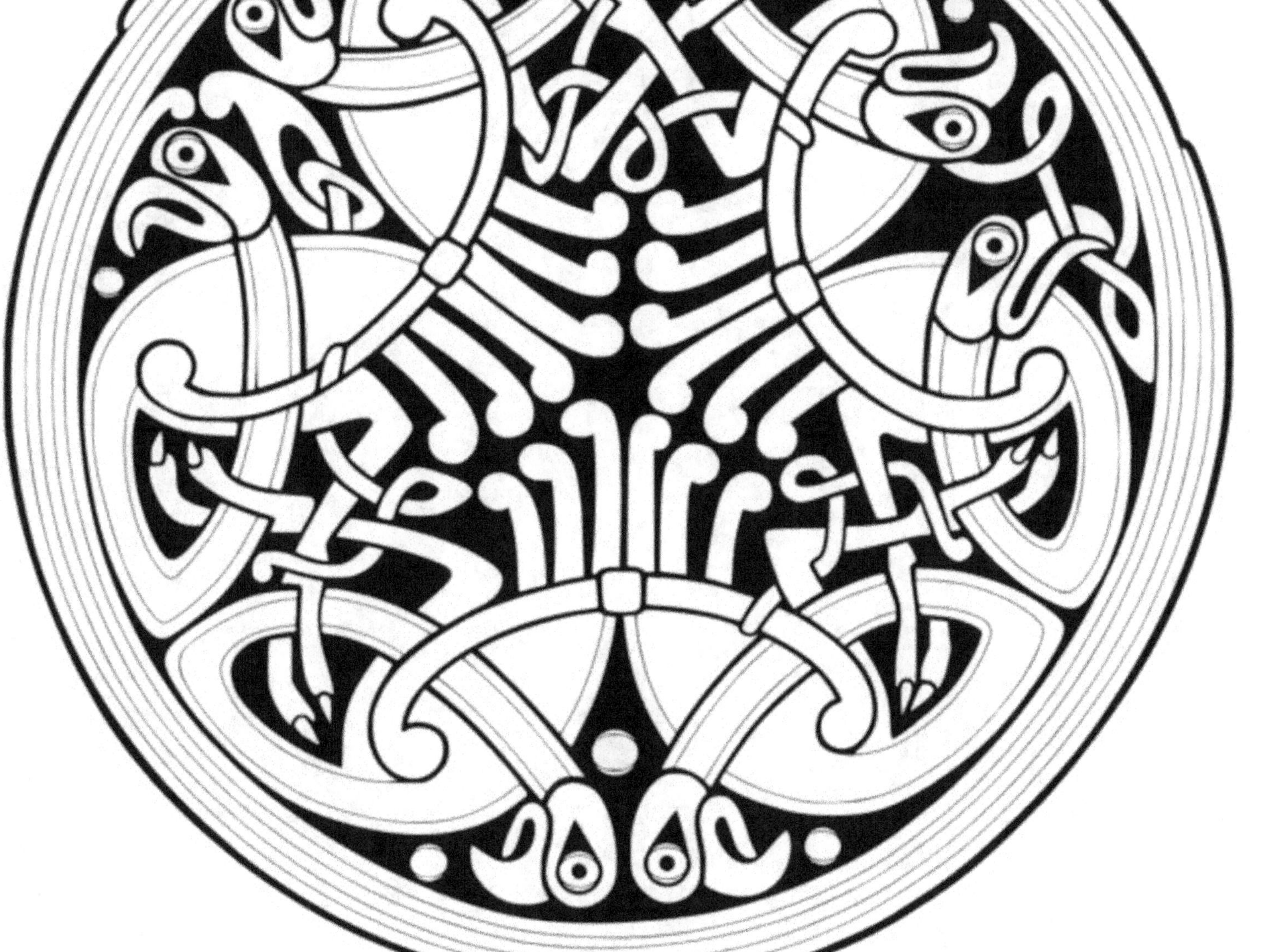

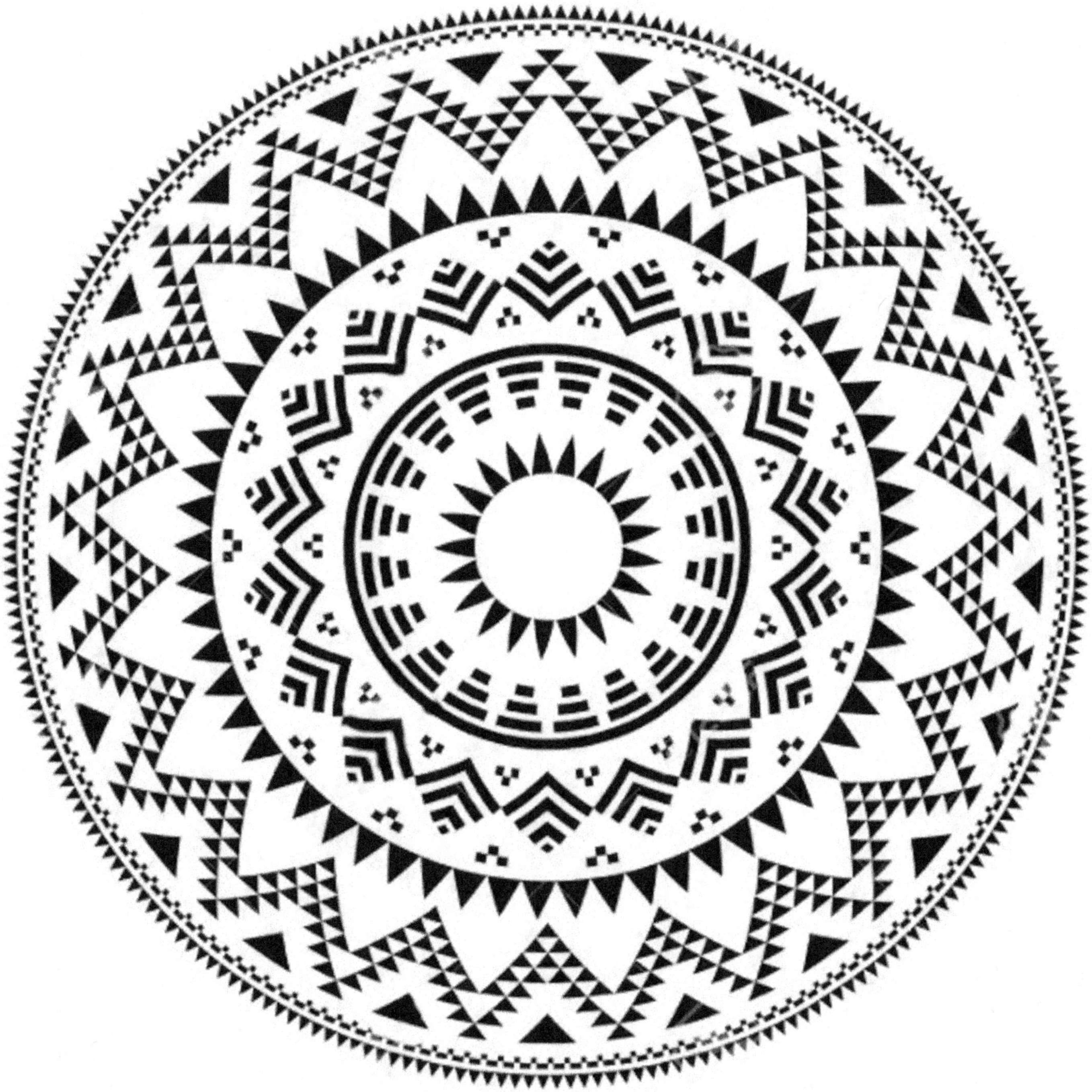

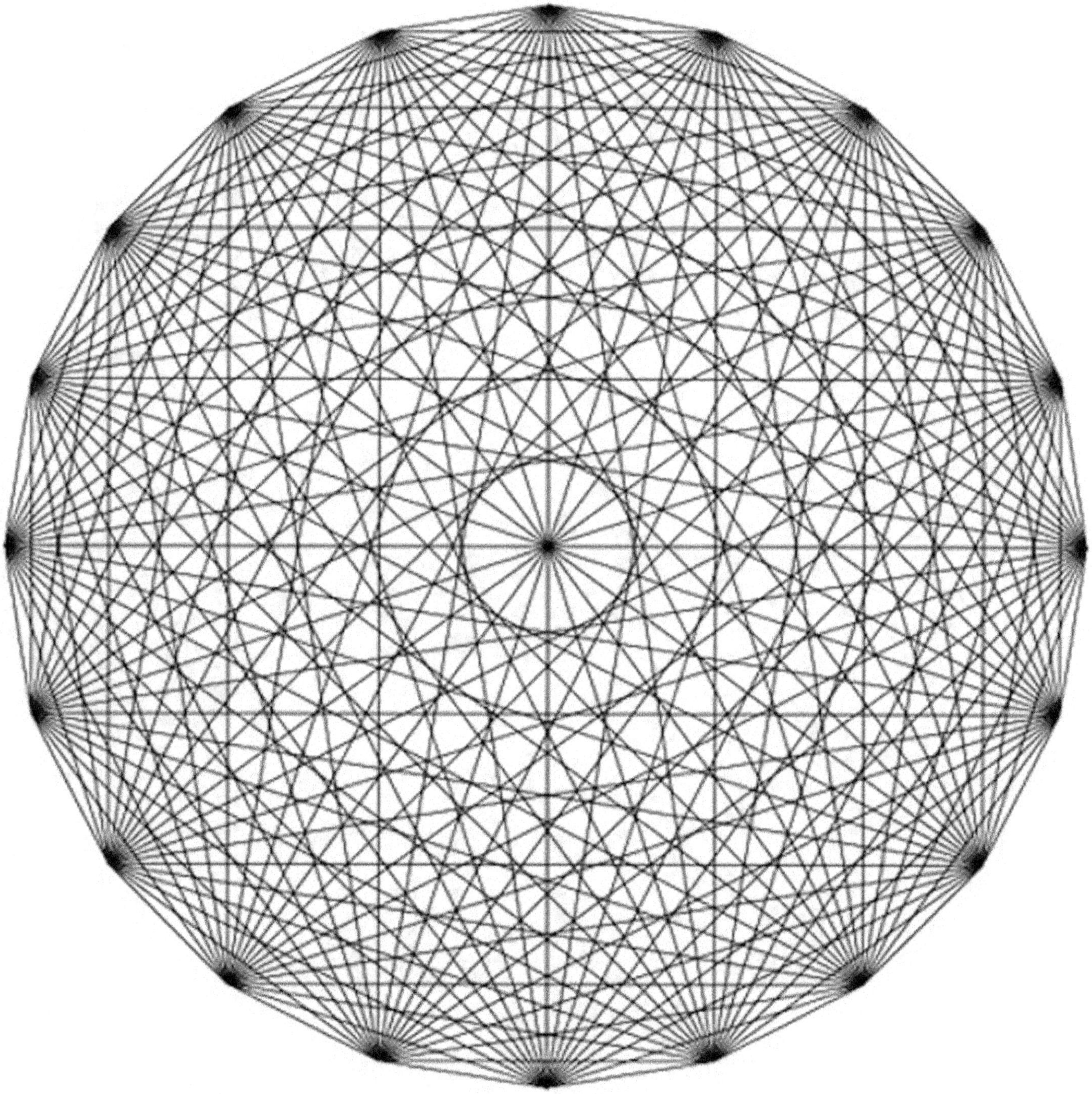

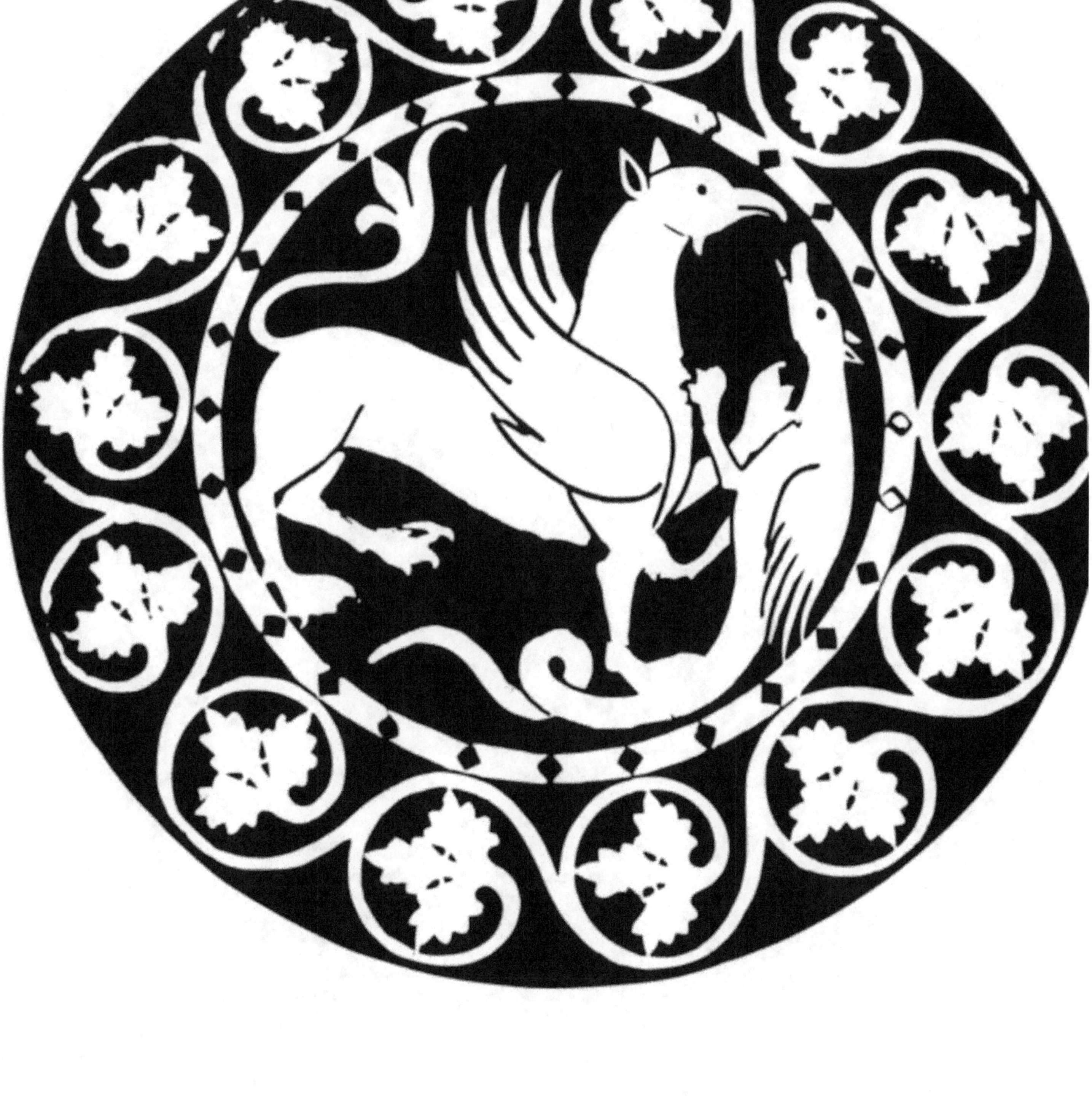

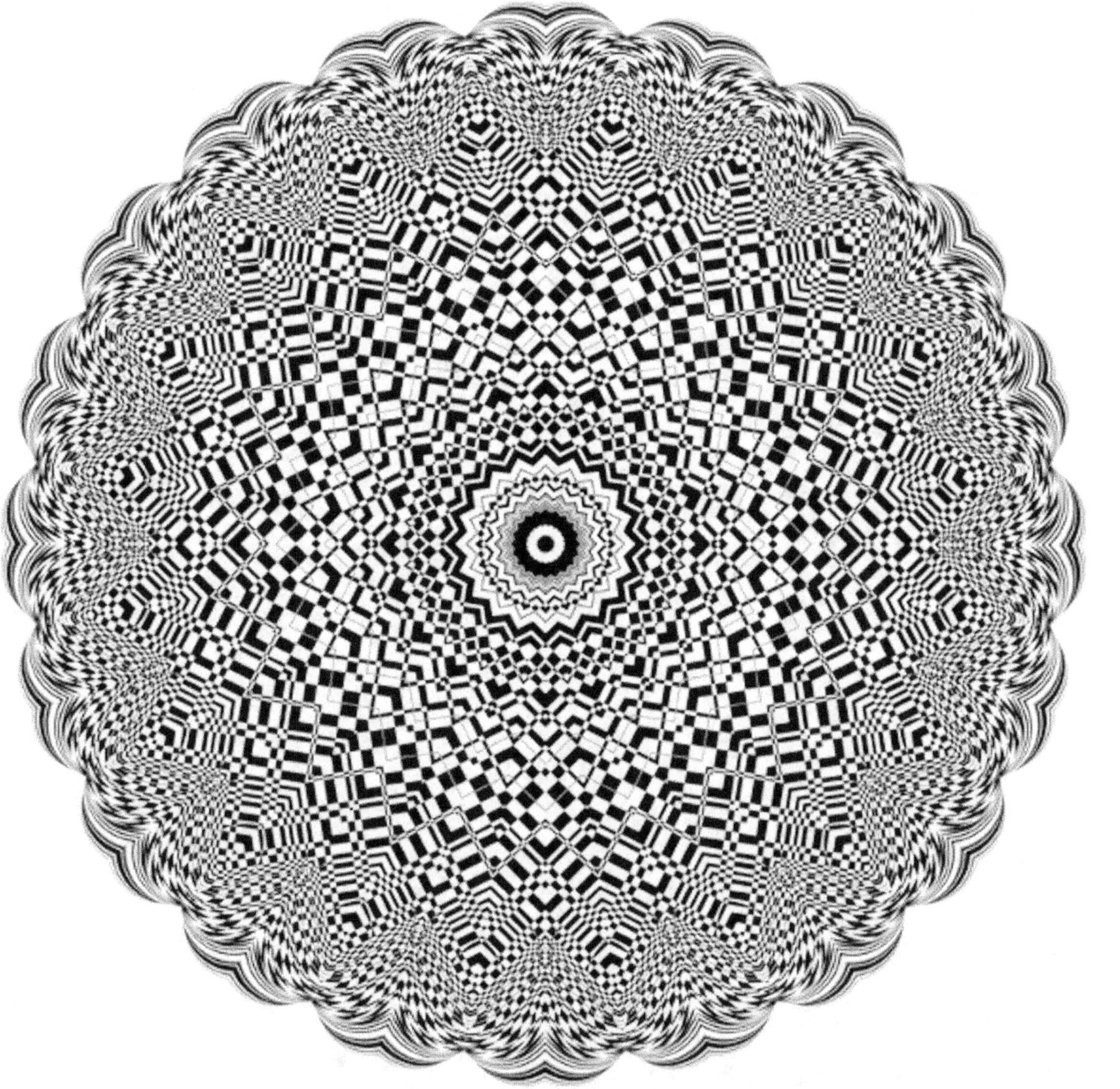

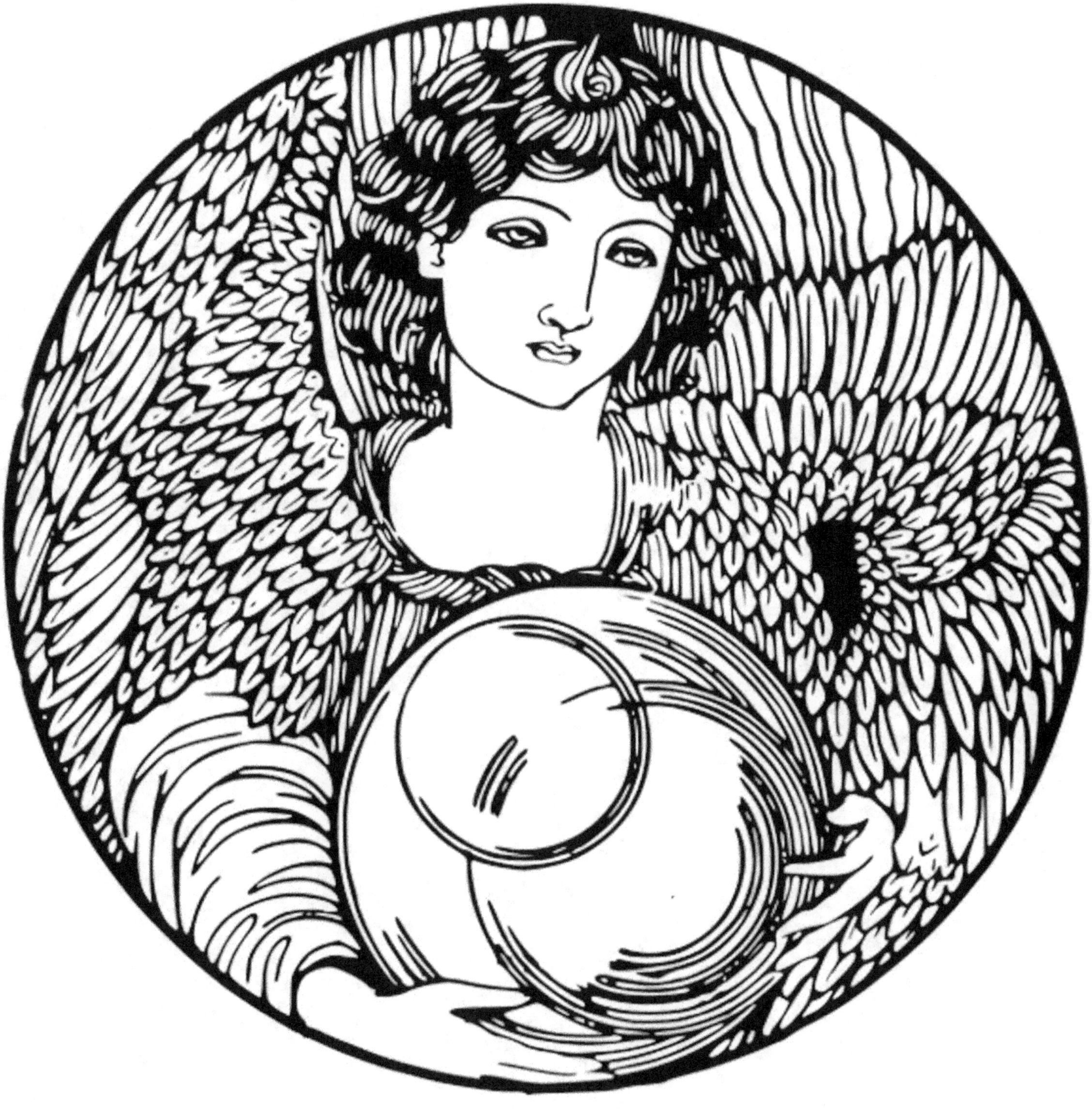

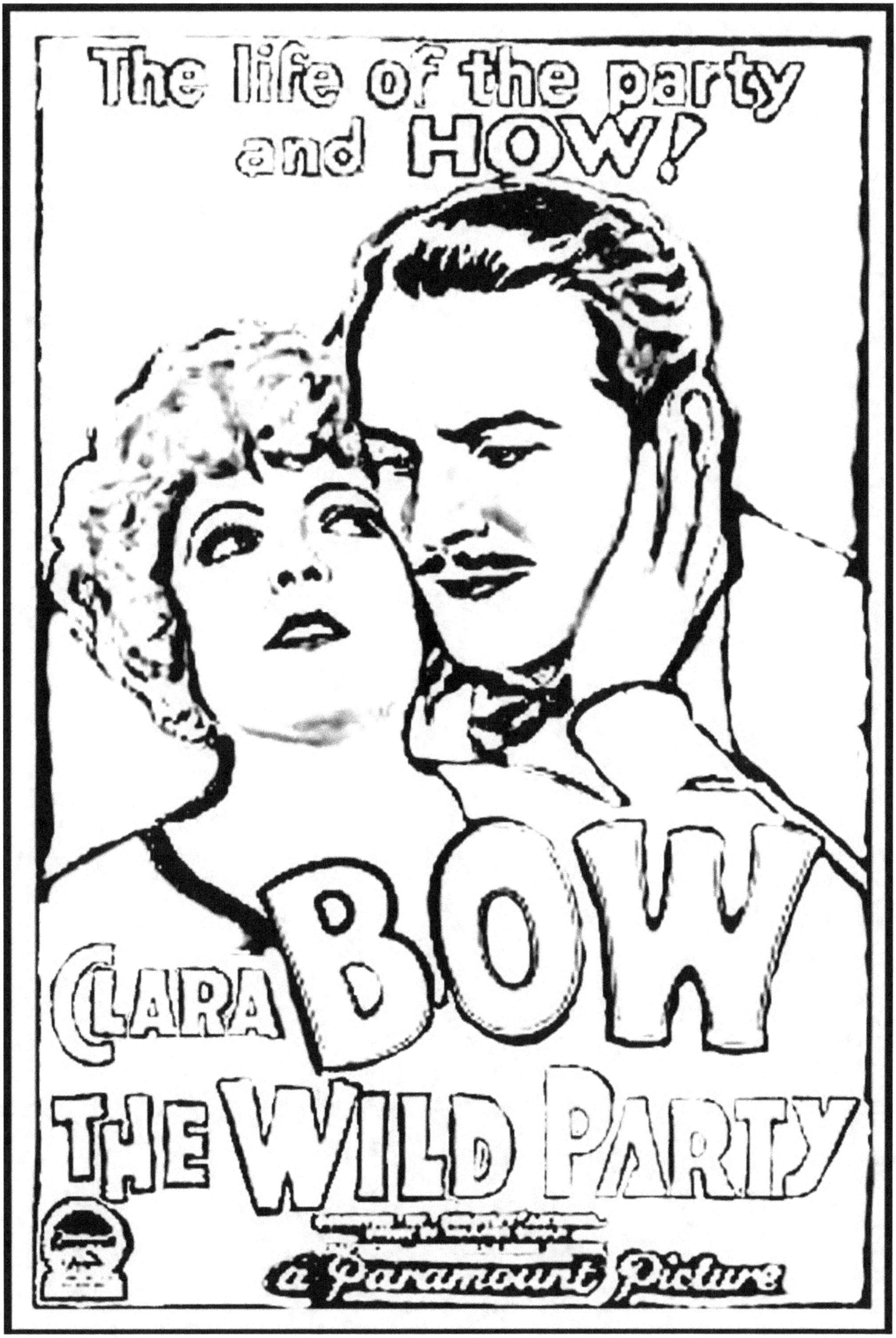
The life of the party
and HOW!
CLARA BOW
THE WILD PARTY
a Paramount Picture

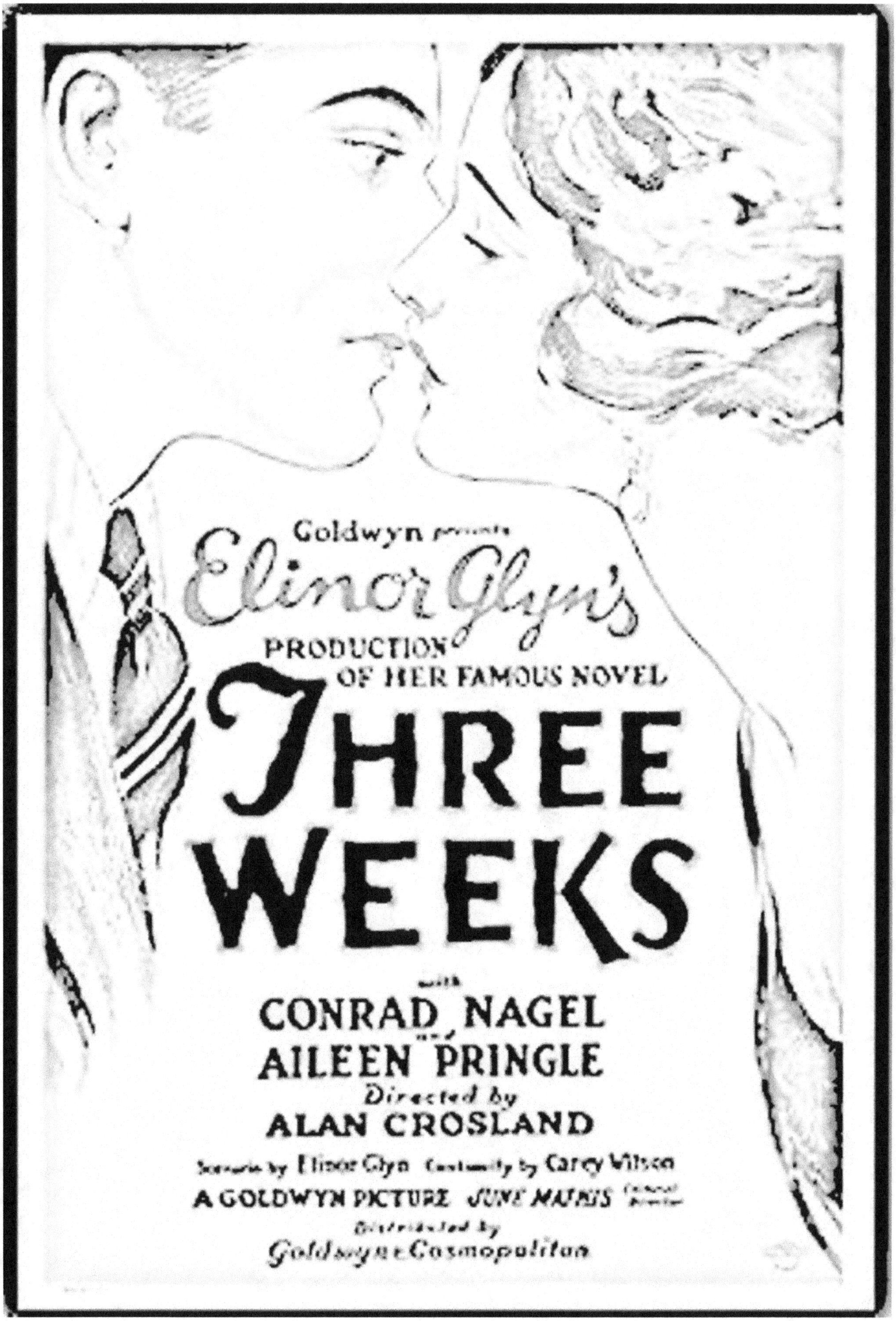

Goldwyn presents
Elinor Glyn's
PRODUCTION
OF HER FAMOUS NOVEL
THREE
WEEKS
with
CONRAD NAGEL
and
AILEEN PRINGLE
Directed by
ALAN CROSLAND
Elinor Glyn
Carey Wilson
A GOLDWYN PICTURE
JUNE MATHIS
Distributed by
Goldwyn Cosmopolitan

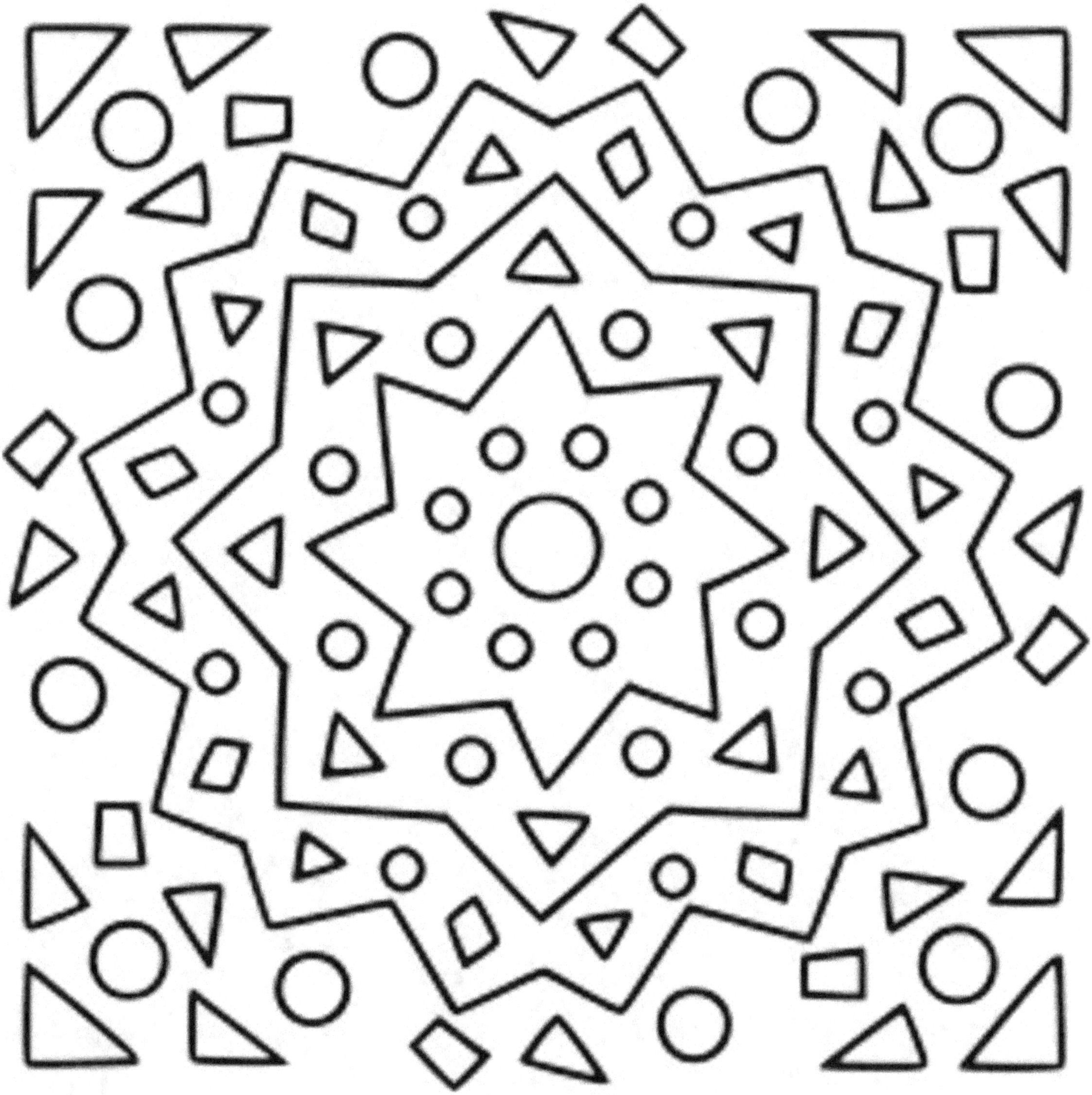

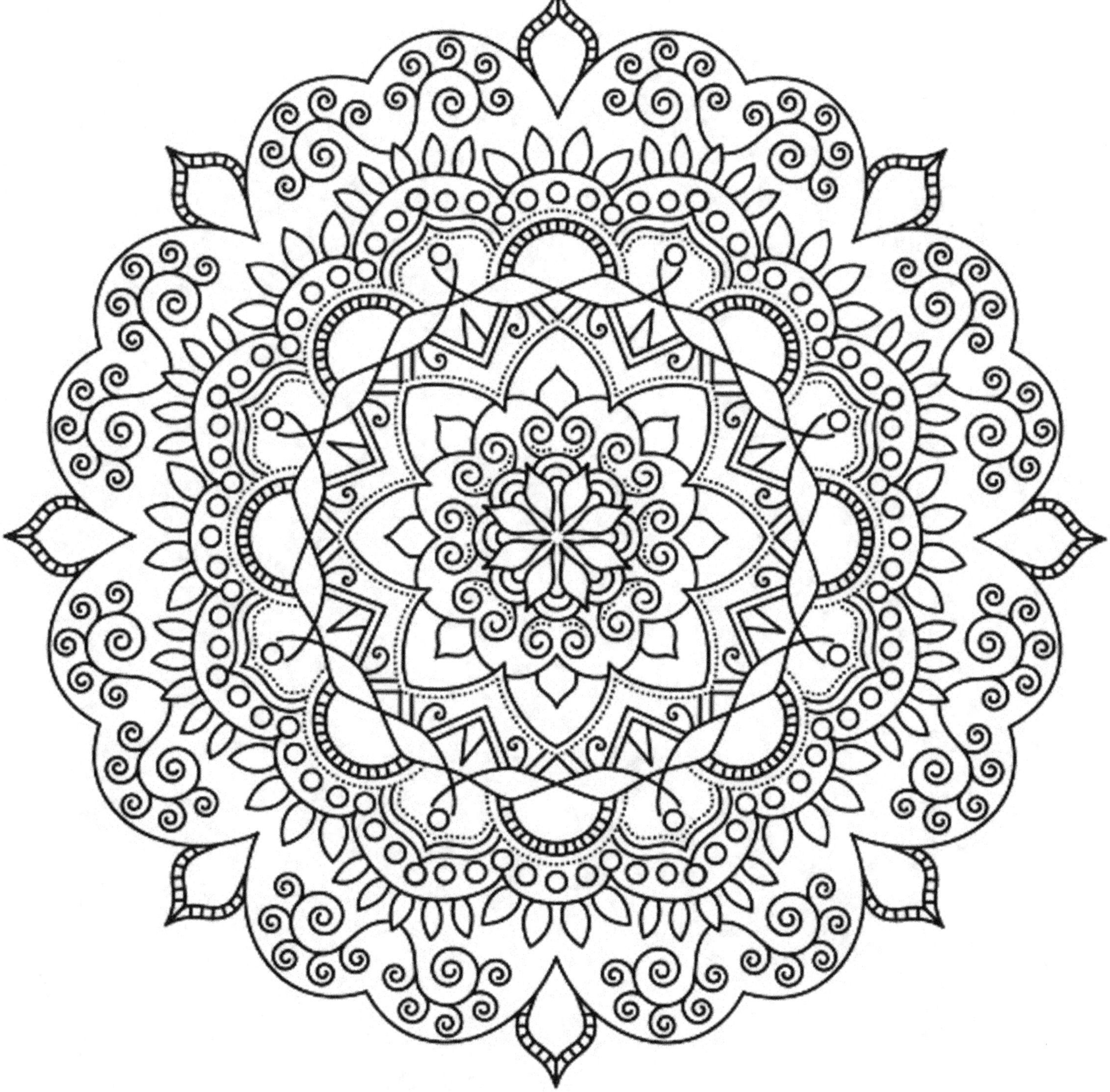

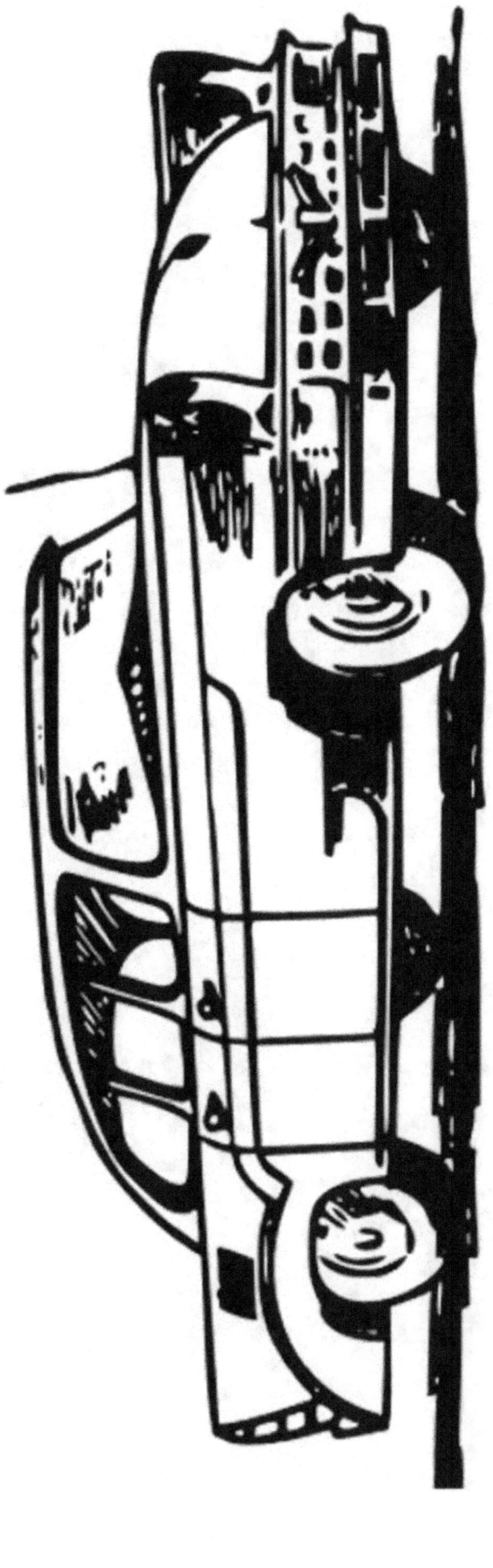

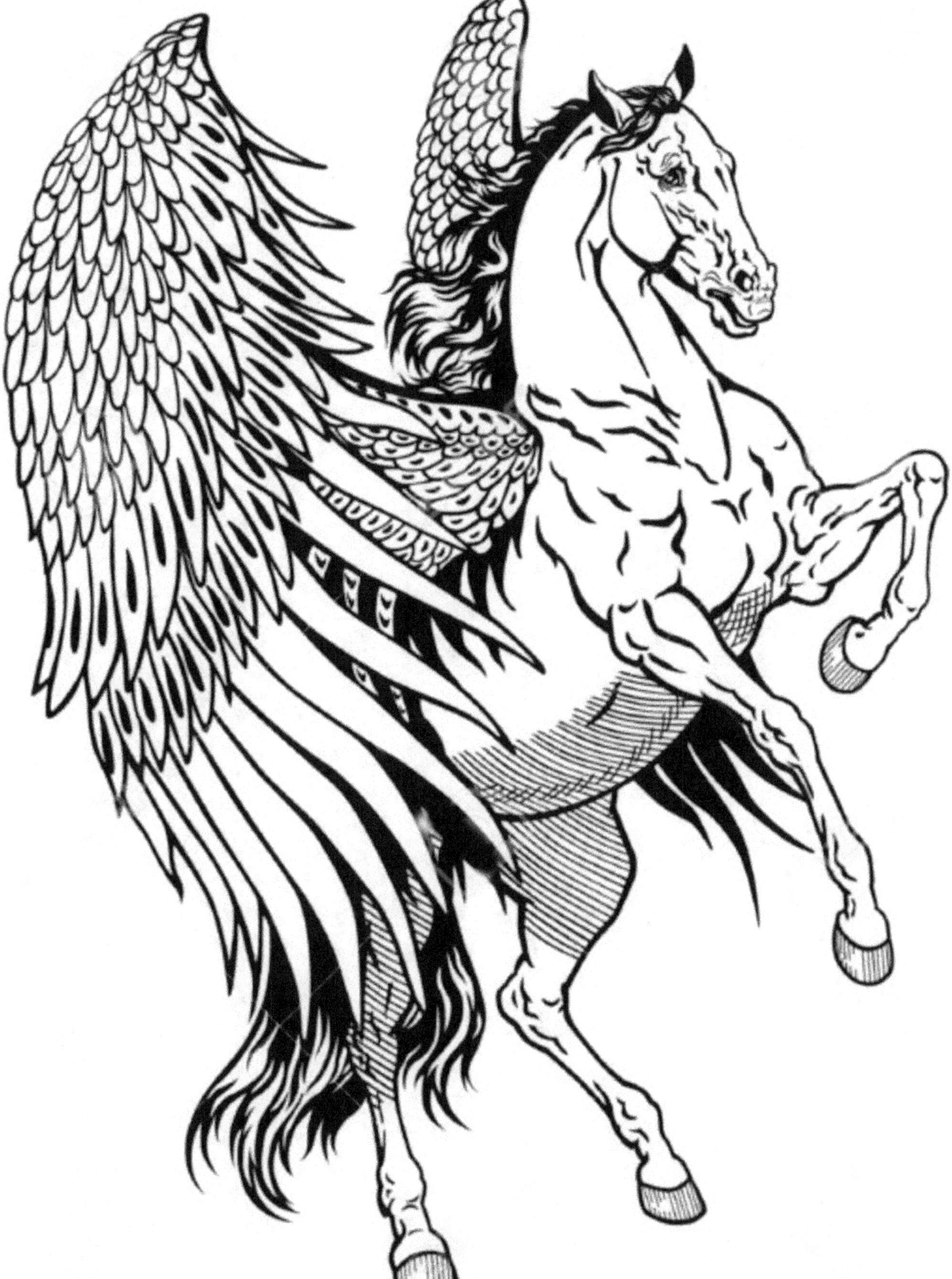

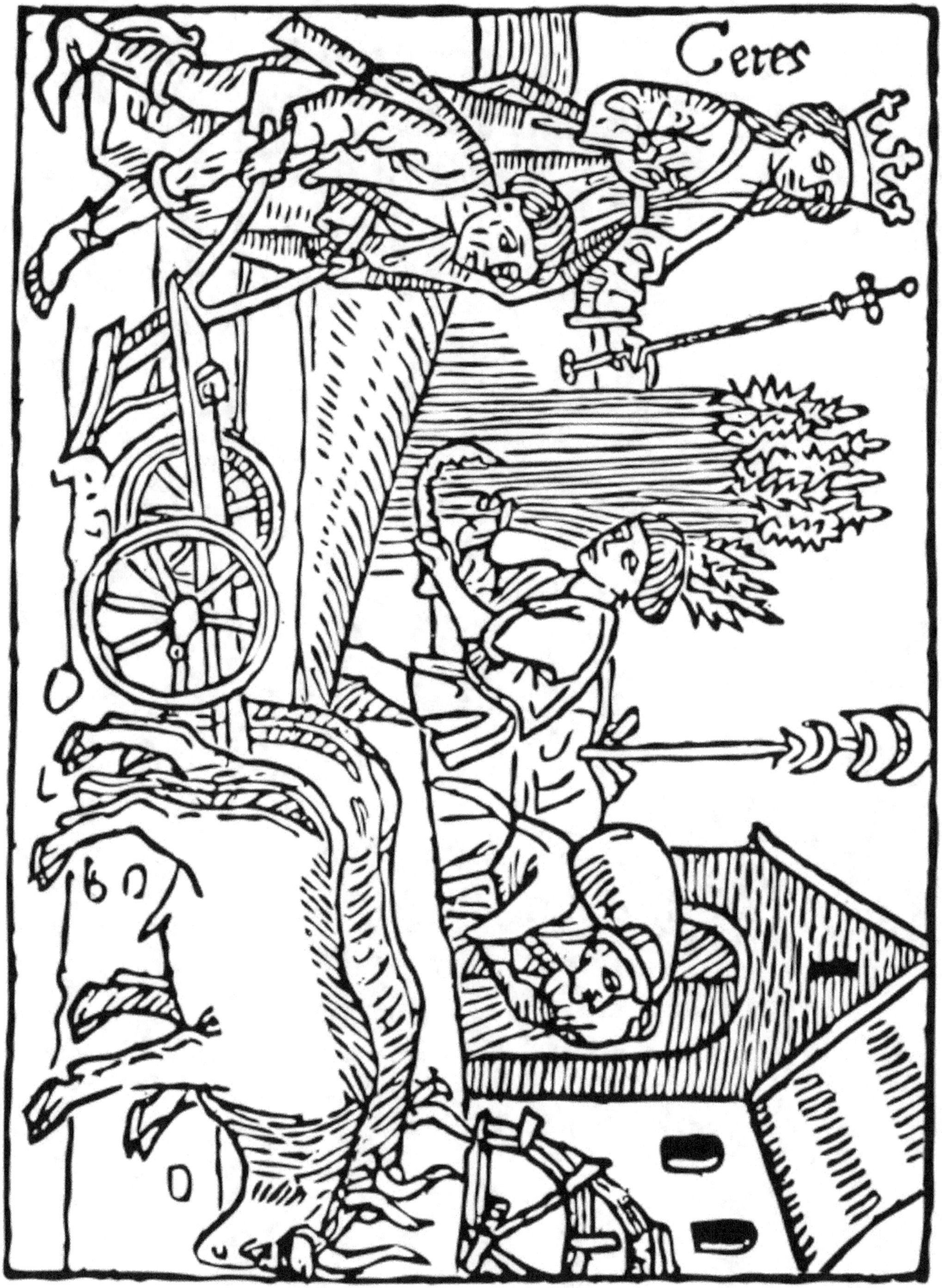
Ceres

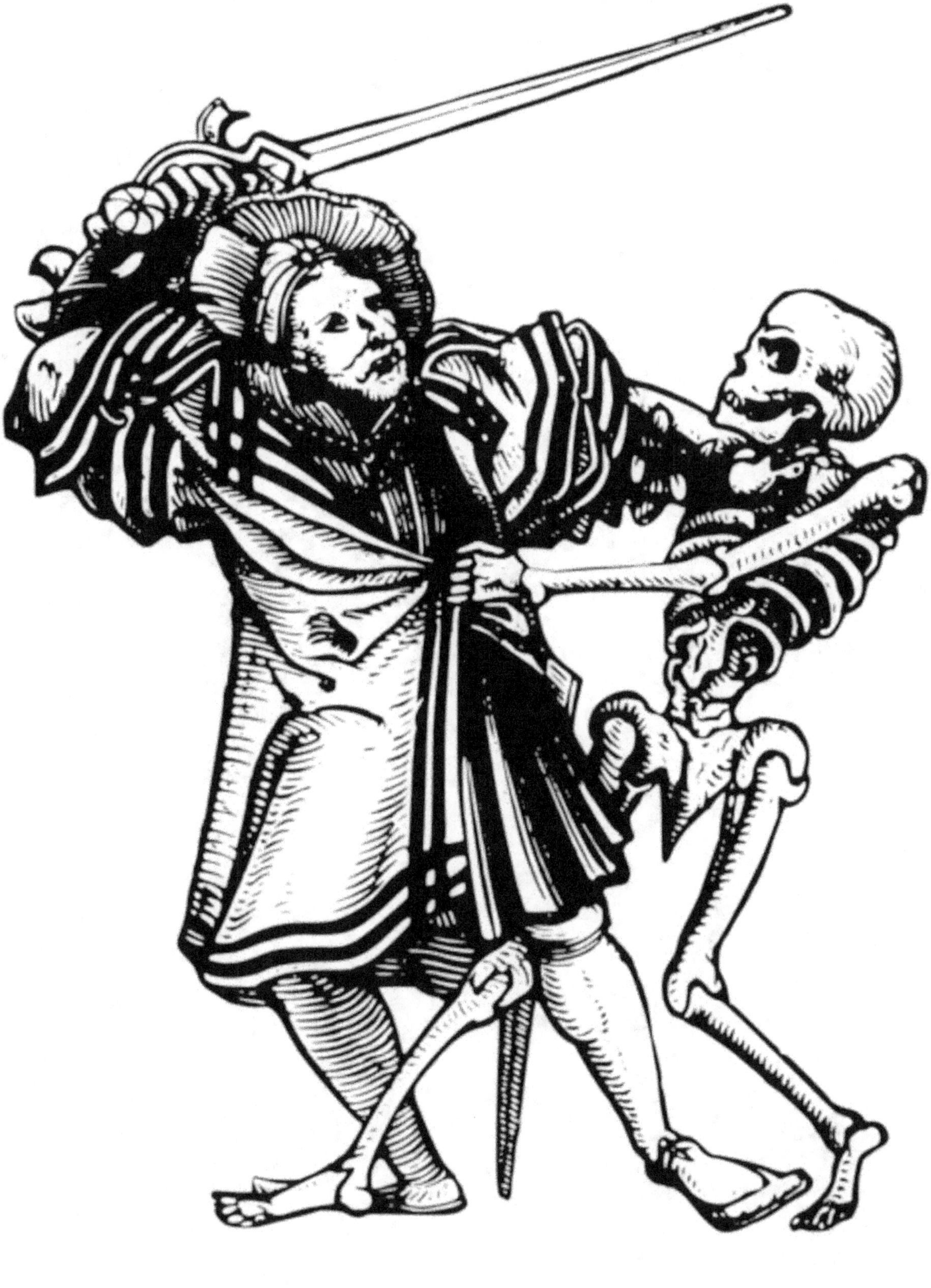

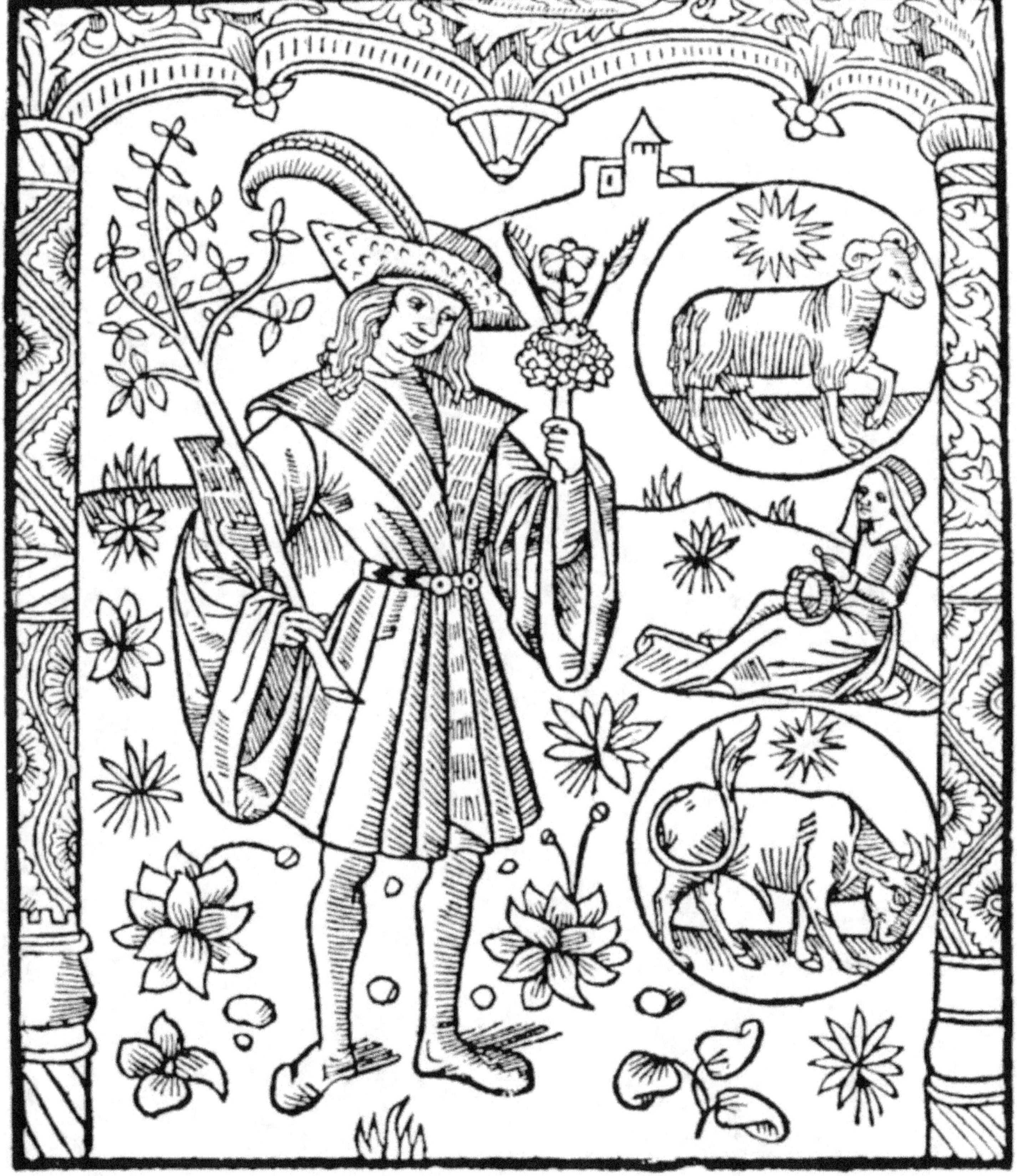

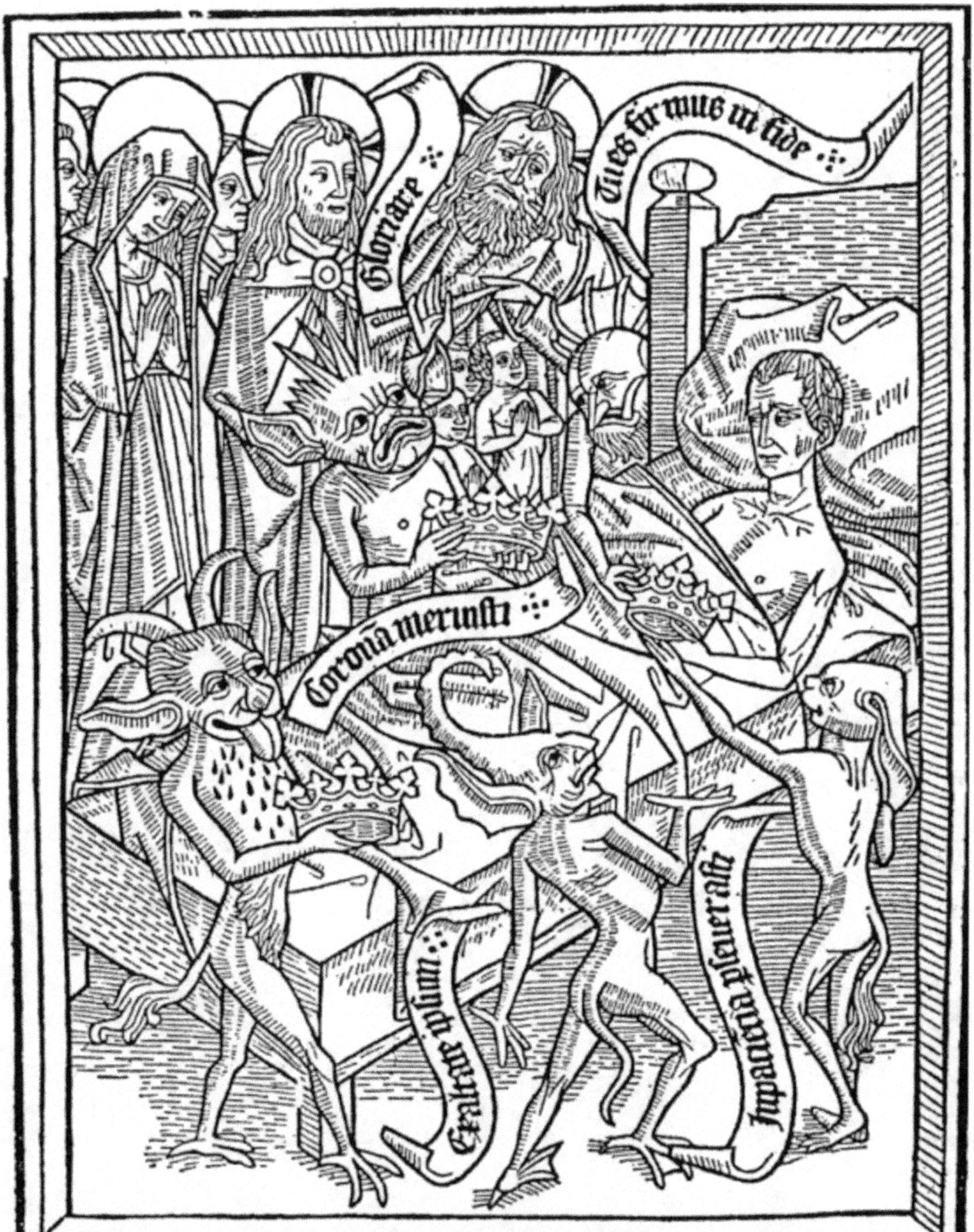
Gloriare
Tu es firmus in fide
Corona meruisti

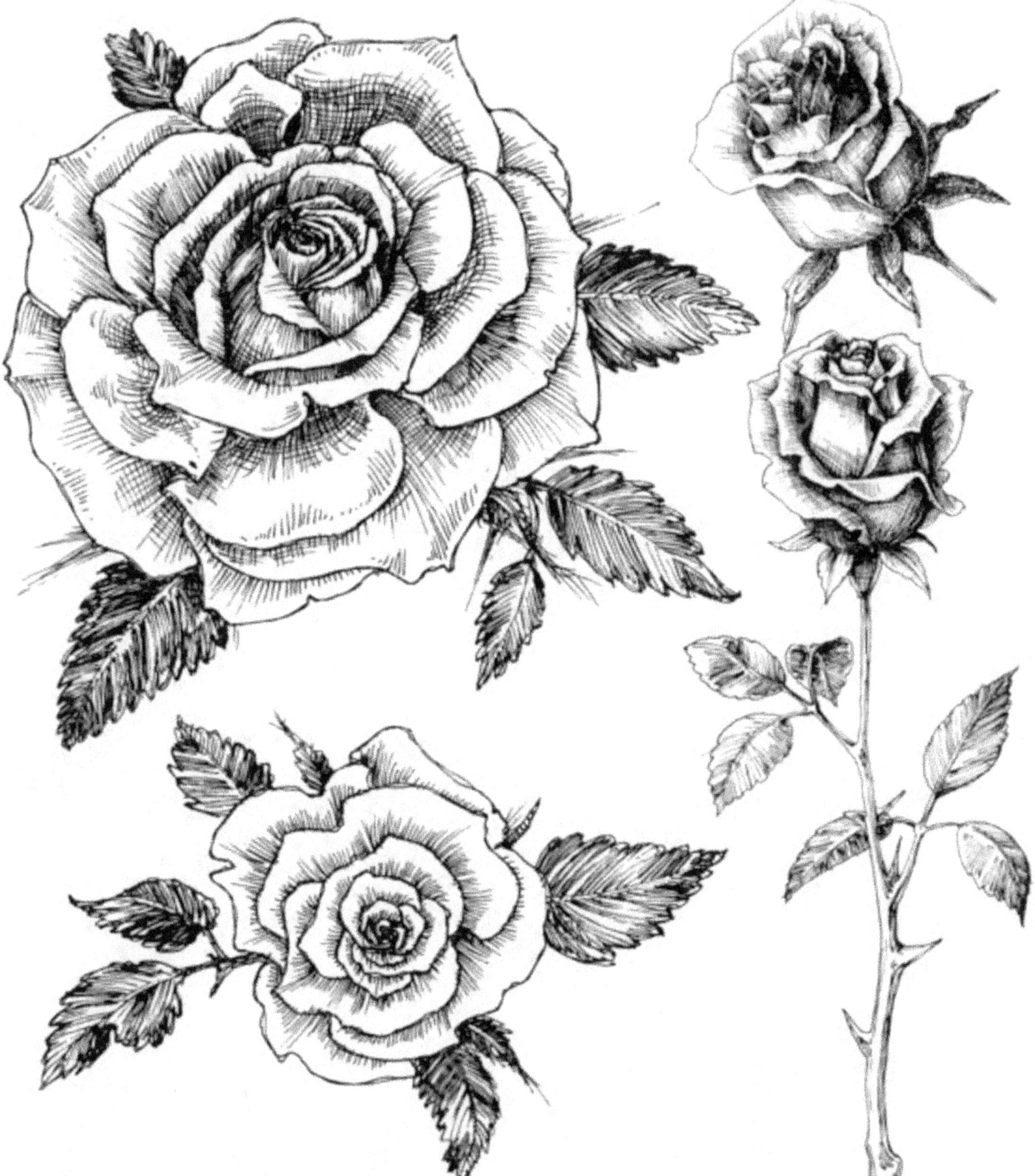

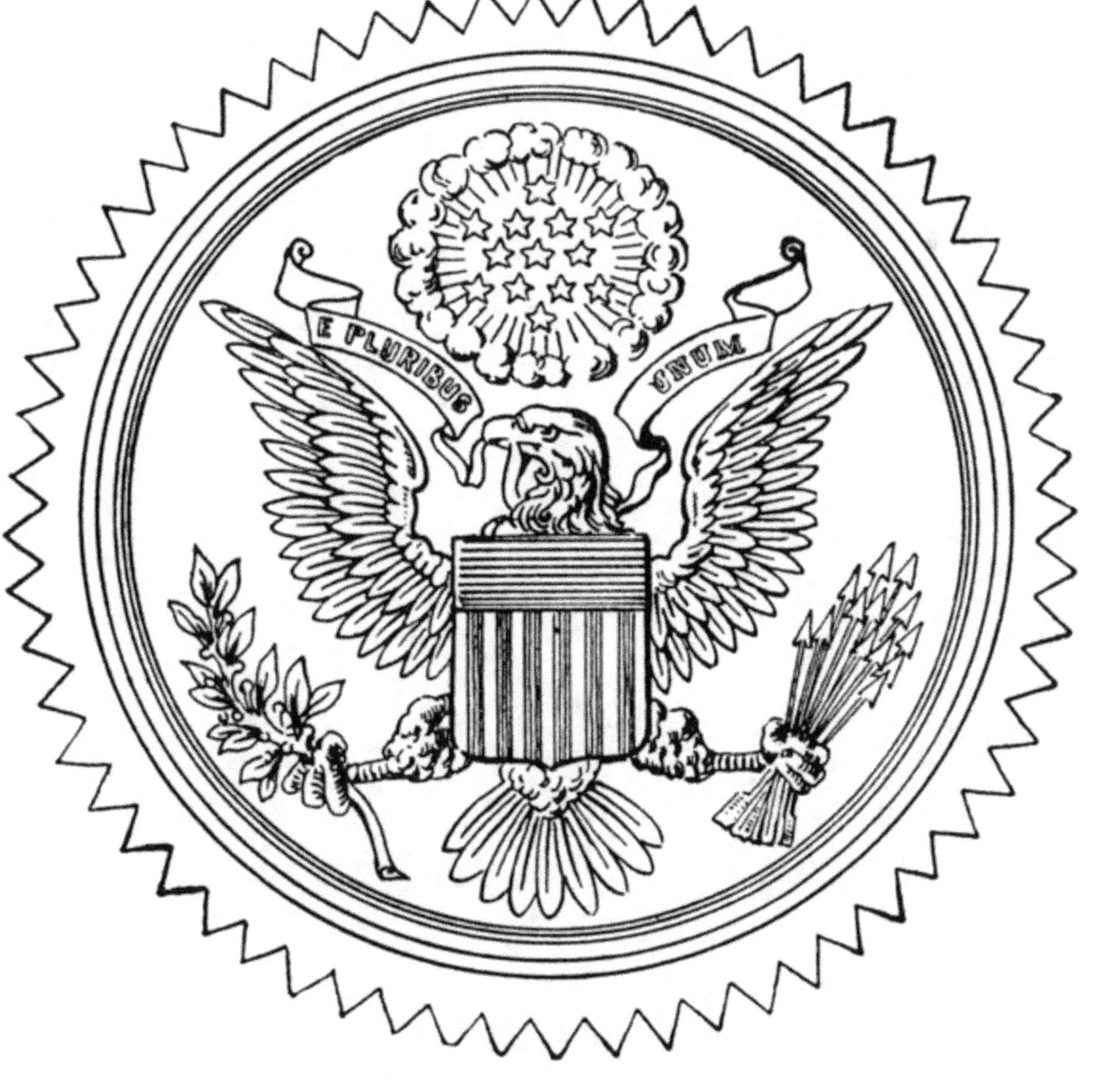
E PLURIBUS
UNUM

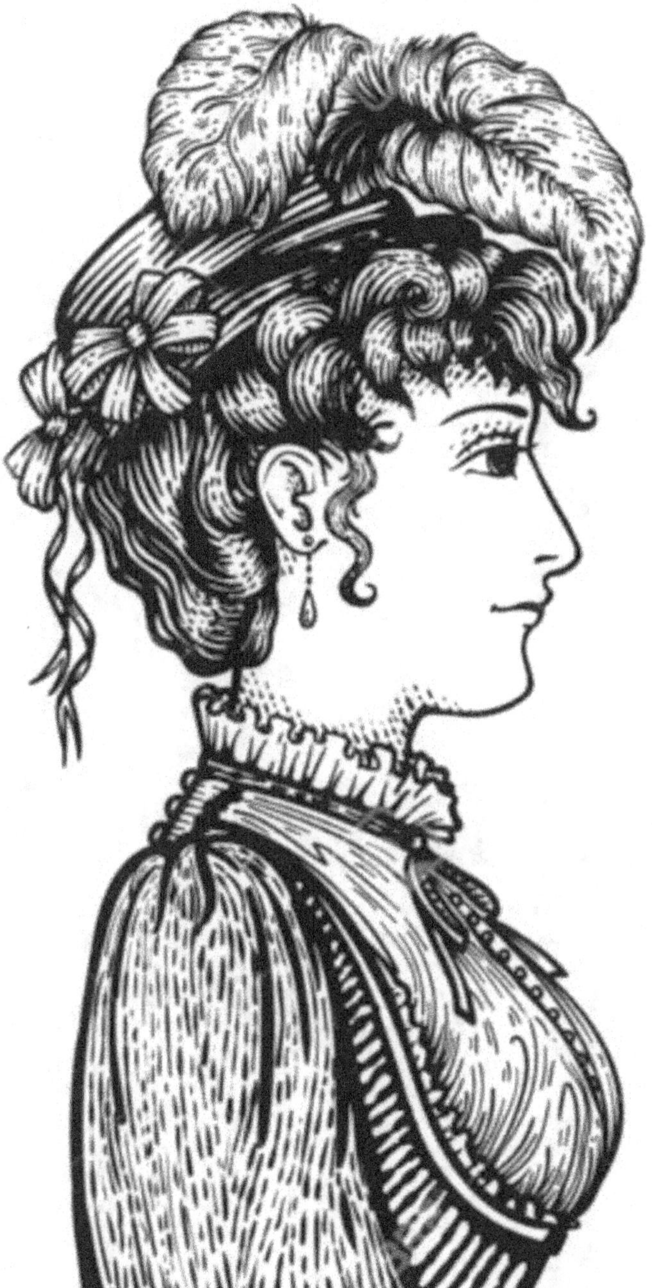

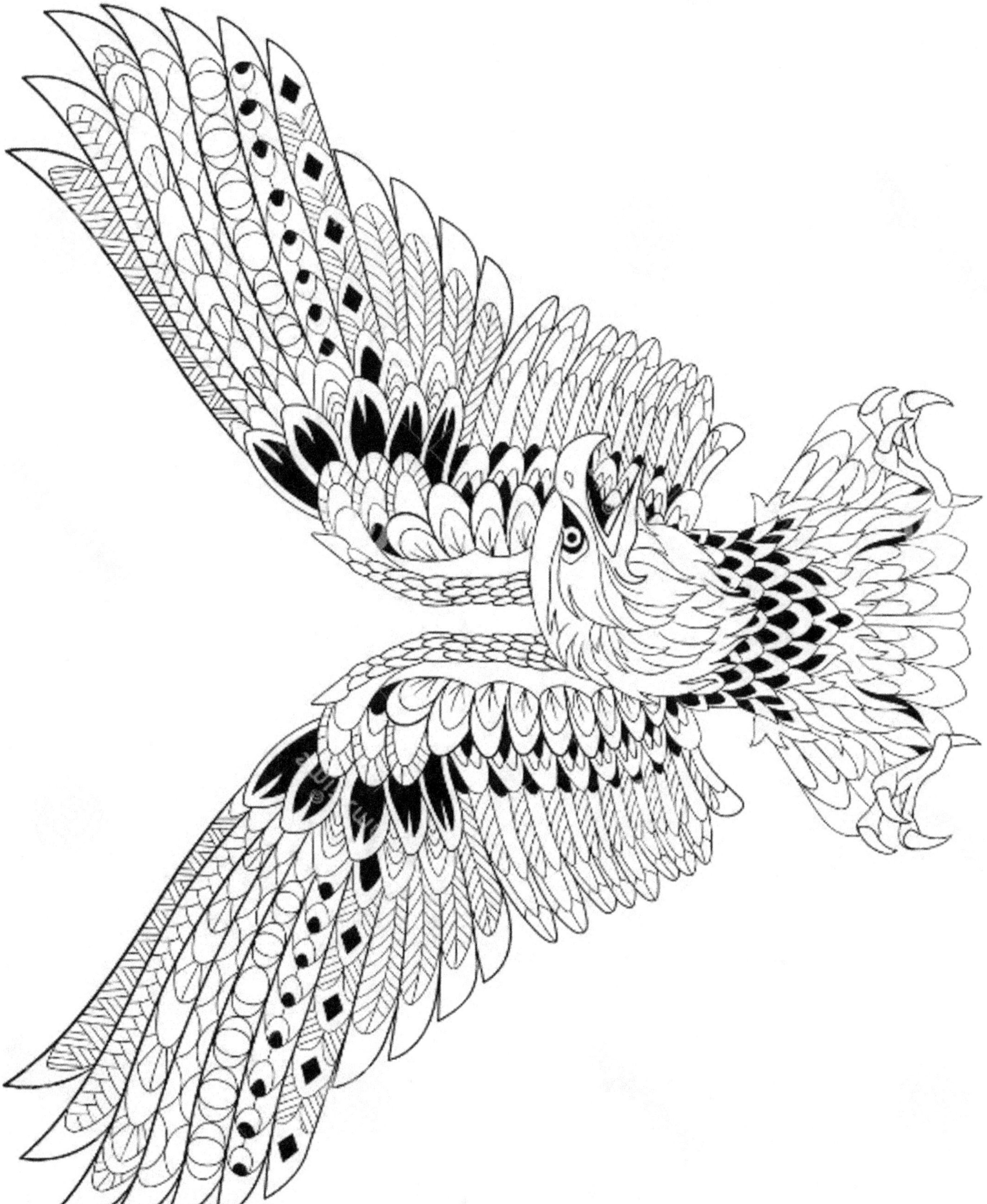

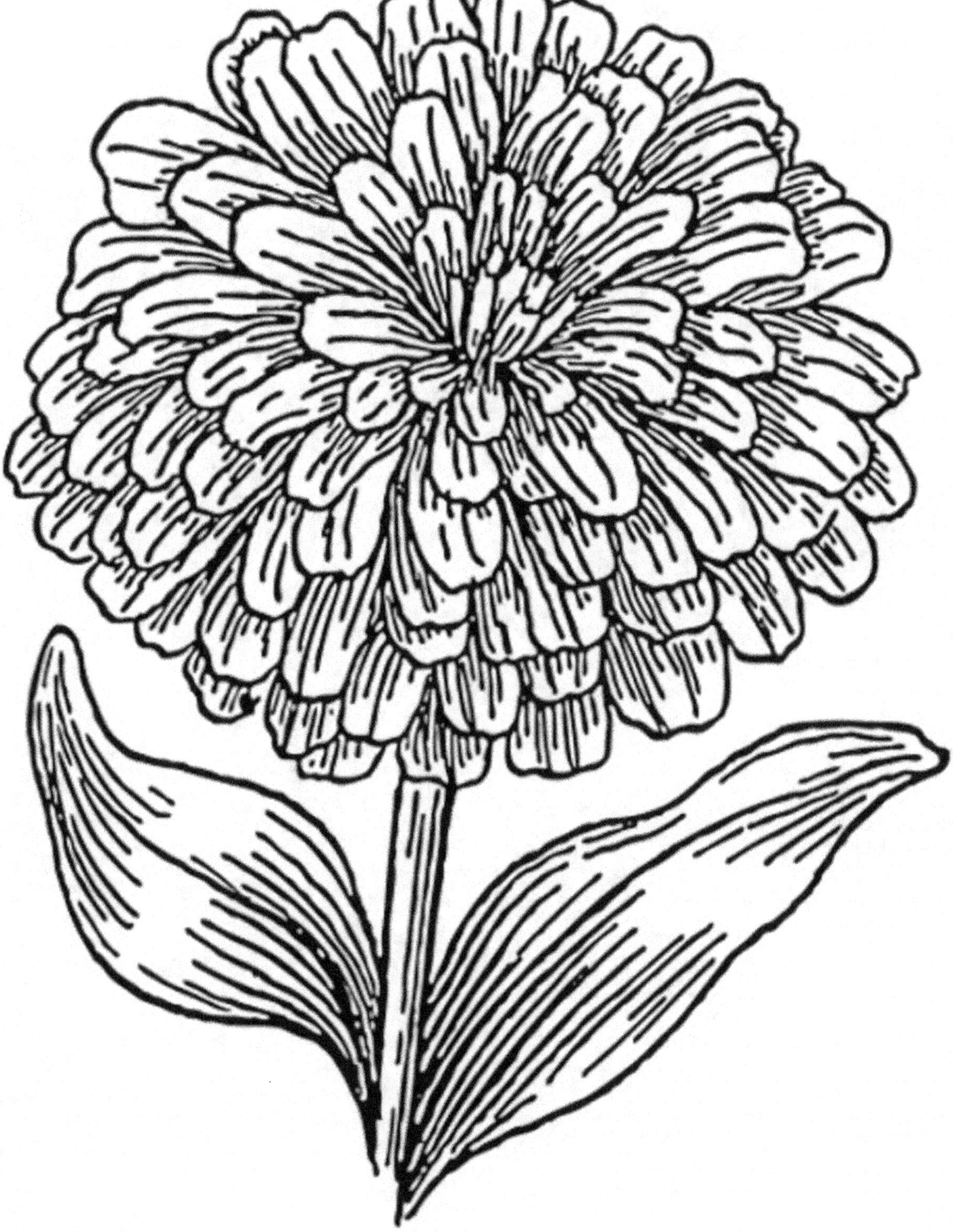

www.ingramcontent.com/pod-product-compliance
Lightning Source LLC
Chambersburg PA
CBHW081742220526
45468CB00008B/2210
9781792652752